ETFs, dangerous financial instruments?

Contents

Contents... 1
Preface... **6**
Disclaimer... **7**
   Notice and Liability.. 7
1. Introduction... **8**
   1.1 What is an ETF?... 8
   1.2 History of ETFs: Rises and Falls... 9
      The ETFs That Didn't Work... 9
      ETFs that have made a lot of money.. 10
   1.3. Differences between ETFs and other funds (mutual, closed, etc.).....11
Part I: ETF Fundamentals.. **14**
   2. How ETFs Work.. 14
      2.1 Structures and Types of ETFs... 14
      2.2. Creation and Redemption Mechanisms................................ 15
      2.3. Roles of Authorized Participants... 17
   3. Advantages of ETFs... 19
      3.1 Diversification and Accessibility... 19
      3.2 Transparency and Liquidity... 21
      3.3 Tax Efficiency.. 23
Part II: The Risks of ETFs.. **26**
   4. Market Risk.. 26
      4.1 Market Volatility and Fluctuations.. 26
      4.2 Leverage and Inverse ETFs.. 28
   5. Tracking Risk (Tracking Error).. 29
      5.1 Tracking Errors and Performance..29
      5.2 Concrete Examples of Significant Tracking Errors................ 31
   6. Liquidity Risk.. 33
      6.1 Liquidity Issues in Volatile Markets.. 33

7. Counterparty Risk.. 36
   7.1 Implications of Trading in Derivatives and Synthetic Products..... 36
   7.2 Case Study on Counterparty Risks.. 38
8. Regulatory Risk... 40
   8.1 Current Regulatory Framework and its Limits............................ 40
   8.2 Regulatory Uncertainties and Potential Impacts........................ 42

Part III: Case Study and Analyzes... 44
9. ETFs and Cryptocurrencies... 44
   9.1 Analysis of Crypto ETFs: Opportunities and Dangers................ 44
   9.2 Specific cases: Bitcoin and Ethereum ETFs............................. 46
10. Catastrophe ETF: Case Studies... 48
   10.1 Detailed analysis of failed ETFs... 48
   10.2 Lessons Learned from Closures and Substantial Losses.......... 50

Part IV: Strategies and Recommendations.................................... 53
11. Evaluation of ETFs... 53
   11.1 Selection criteria for investors.. 53
   11.2 Tools and resources for evaluating ETFs................................ 55
12. Portfolio Management Strategies... 57
   12.1 Integration of ETFs into a diversified portfolio........................ 57
   12.2 Approaches to limiting the risks associated with ETFs............ 59
13. Alternatives to ETFs.. 61
   13.1 Comparison with traditional funds and other financial products. 61
   13.2 Advantages and disadvantages of alternatives...................... 63

Part V: Advanced Strategies and Emerging Trends........................ 66
14. Smart Beta and Factor Investing.. 66
   14.1 Understanding Smart Beta ETFs.. 66
   14.2 How Factor Investing Works.. 67
   14.3 Examples and Performance Analysis..................................... 67
      Conclusion.. 68
15. Environmental, Social, and Governance (ESG) ETFs.......... 68
   15.1 What Are ESG ETFs?... 68
   Conclusion... 70
   15.2 Growing Popularity and Impact.. 70

- 15.3 Case Studies of Successful ESG ETFs.................................73
  - Conclusion..75
- 16. Thematic Investing with ETFs...75
  - 16.1 Introduction to Thematic ETFs...................................... 76
  - Conclusion..78
  - 16.2 Popular Themes: Technology, Healthcare, Green Energy......... 78
  - 16.3 Risks and Opportunities.. 80
- 17. Sector and Industry ETFs.. 83
  - 17.1 Overview of Sector-Specific ETFs..................................83
  - Conclusion..85
  - 17.2 Performance and Risk Analysis.....................................85
  - Conclusion..88
  - 17.3 Integration into Investment Portfolios......................... 88
- 18. ETFs in Retirement Accounts... 90
  - 18.1 Benefits of ETFs in Retirement Accounts.....................91
  - Conclusion..93
  - 18.2 Strategies for Long-Term Growth................................. 93
  - Conclusion..96
  - 18.3 Tax Advantages and Considerations............................. 96
  - Conclusion..99
- 19. Leveraged and Inverse ETFs..99
  - 19.1 How They Work... 99
  - Conclusion.. 101
  - 19.2 Risks and Rewards...101
  - Conclusion.. 104
  - 19.3 Suitability for Different Types of Investors................ 104
  - Conclusion.. 106

Part VI: Practical Applications... 107
- 20. Building a Portfolio with ETFs... 107
  - 20.1 Step-by-Step Guide to Portfolio Construction............107
  - Conclusion.. 109
  - 20.2 Sample Portfolios for Different Risk Profiles............. 110
  - Conclusion.. 113

- 20.3 Rebalancing and Monitoring Your Portfolio 113
  - Conclusion 115
- 21. ETFs in Different Market Conditions 116
  - 21.1 Strategies for Bull and Bear Markets 116
  - Conclusion 118
  - 21.2 Using ETFs for Hedging and Risk Management 119
  - Conclusion 122
  - 21.3 Case Studies of ETFs in Market Crises 123
  - Conclusion 125
- 22. Global ETFs and International Diversification 125
  - 22.1 Benefits of International Exposure 126
  - Conclusion 127
  - 22.2 Types of Global ETFs 128
  - Conclusion 130
  - 22.3 Risks and Considerations 131
  - Conclusion 134
- 23. Tax-Loss Harvesting with ETFs 135
  - 23.1 What is Tax-Loss Harvesting? 135
  - 23.2 How to Implement It with ETFs 136
  - Conclusion 139
  - 23.3 Benefits and Pitfalls 139
  - Conclusion 141
- 24. Understanding ETF Fees and Expenses 142
  - 24.1 Different Types of Fees 142
  - Conclusion 144
  - 24.2 Impact on Long-Term Returns 144
  - Conclusion 146
  - 24.3 Comparing ETF Costs 147
  - Conclusion : Practical Applications 149

Conclusion 150
- 25. ETFs: Final Thoughts 150
  - 25.1 Summary of benefits and risks 150
  - 25.2 Future Outlook of ETFs 151

Annexes **154**
   26. Glossary of Key Terms 154
   27. Additional Resources 156
   28. Bibliography 158

ETFs, dangerous financial instruments?

Preface

It is with great pleasure that we present to you "ETFs, dangerous financial instruments?" by Tanguy Blis. This book is an in-depth and nuanced exploration of Exchange Traded Funds (ETFs), a modern investment tool that has transformed the global financial landscape. Tanguy Blis, with his experience and passion for financial markets, offers us here a detailed analysis of the advantages and risks associated with ETFs.

Tanguy Blis' objective is not to dictate absolute truths, but to provide readers with the keys to understanding and navigating the complex world of ETFs. Through concrete examples, rigorous analyzes and a touch of humor, he seeks to demystify these financial instruments to allow everyone to make informed decisions.

In this book, you will learn not only how ETFs work, but also tracking errors, liquidity issues and many other critical aspects. Tanguy Blis invites each reader to question, reflect and deepen their knowledge, emphasizing the importance of prudence and financial education.

We hope this book will inspire and enlighten you, while highlighting the need to diversify your sources of information and consult experts before making investment decisions. Ultimately, "Are ETFs dangerous financial instruments?" is an invitation to explore with curiosity and discernment the fascinating world of ETFs.

The Editor

Disclaimer

Notice and Liability

The author, Tanguy Blis, would like to clarify that the opinions expressed in this book only represent his personal point of view and are based on his experience and research. The examples and analyzes presented are provided for informational and educational purposes only. It should not be considered specific financial, legal or investment advice.

The author may be wrong, and it is crucial for readers not to make investment decisions based solely on the content of this book. Any financial decision should be made after consulting multiple sources and qualified professionals to adequately evaluate risks and opportunities.

The aim of this book is to make a modest contribution to the search for truth and to provide an informed perspective on Exchange Traded Funds (ETFs). However, the author assumes no responsibility for the accuracy, completeness or suitability of the information contained in this book. Readers are urged to use their best judgment and conduct their own thorough research before making any investment decisions.

1. Introduction

In our perpetual quest for a better understanding of financial instruments, today we turn to Exchange Traded Funds, or ETFs. These modern portfolio management tools, both ingenious and complex, deserve our attention and rigorous analysis. They embody economic and financial progress, offering diversified and accessible investment opportunities. However, it is essential to examine them with a discerning eye and an open mind, seeking to understand both their promise and their potential perils.

1.1 What is an ETF?

An ETF, or Exchange Traded Fund, is a type of investment that combines the simplicity of individual stocks with the diversification of mutual funds. Simply put, an ETF is a fund that holds a basket of assets – stocks, bonds, commodities, or others – and whose shares are traded on a stock exchange. This mechanism allows investors to buy and sell shares of the fund throughout the trading day, just as they would with ordinary shares.

The story of ETFs begins in the late 1980s, a period marked by dynamic financial innovation and a growing need for flexibility and lower cost in investments. The first ETF, known as the SPDR S&P 500 ETF Trust (ticker: SPY), was launched in 1993. This fund aimed to track the performance of the S&P 500 Index, providing investors with diversified exposure to major American companies with the liquidity of a share.

Since this first launch, the ETF market has experienced extraordinary expansion. Today, there are thousands of ETFs covering a wide range of asset classes, economic sectors, and investment strategies. Their popularity is based on several key advantages: diversification, transparency, liquidity and tax efficiency. These characteristics make ETFs powerful tools for individual and institutional investors seeking to optimize their portfolios.

However, as with any financial innovation, it is crucial to consider not only the benefits, but also the potential risks. ETFs can introduce unexpected complexities and volatilities, and their use should be guided by clear and informed understanding. As we continue this exploration, we will seek to uncover the truth about ETFs, carefully weighing their advantages against their disadvantages, with a spirit of discernment and caution.

Ultimately, our goal is to provide a balanced and informed view, enabling everyone to make informed and responsible investment choices. Let's embark together on this journey of discovery, driven by the desire to learn and understand, to navigate with confidence in the fascinating world of Exchange Traded Funds.

***

After exploring what an ETF is, its definition, and its history, it is essential to understand how these financial instruments have performed over the years. The history of ETFs is marked by resounding successes which brought considerable gains to their investors, but also by notorious failures which led to substantial losses. This duality highlights the opportunities and dangers inherent in these financial products.

In this section, we'll take an in-depth look at some notable examples of ETFs that have performed exceptionally well as well as those that have failed spectacularly. By analyzing these cases, we will be able to better understand the success factors and the pitfalls to avoid. This historical and analytical journey will allow us to gain a clearer and nuanced view of ETFs, helping us make more informed investment choices.

1.2 History of ETFs: Rises and Falls

The ETFs That Didn't Work

The history of ETFs is not only made up of brilliant successes. Some funds have failed spectacularly, causing significant losses for investors. These examples serve as valuable warnings and highlight the risks associated with these products.

1. **ARK Innovation ETF (ARKK)** : Initially celebrated for its exposure to technological innovation, the ARKK fund experienced a dramatic fall in 2022. The high concentration in volatile technology stocks led to a loss of 67% of its value, resulting in an erosion of 14.3 billion dollars for its investors (markets.businessinsider.com)[1].
2. **MSCI China All Shares Health Care ETF** : This fund has been seriously affected by strict regulations and economic uncertainty in China. In 2024, it recorded a loss of 62.77%, illustrating the challenges and risks of investing in emerging markets ([ETF portfolios made simple | justETF](https://www.justetf.com))[2].
3. **Global X MSCI SuperDividend EAFE ETF (EFAS)** : Designed to deliver high returns across dividend stocks in Europe and Asia, this fund has underperformed due to the vulnerability of its assets and poor performance in international markets.

ETFs that have made a lot of money

In contrast, some ETFs have reported substantial gains, becoming models of success in the financial world.

1. **Invesco QQQ Trust (QQQ)** : Tracking the Nasdaq-100 Index, this fund benefited from the explosive growth of technology companies like Apple and Microsoft, recording remarkable gains.
2. **SPDR S&P 500 ETF Trust (SPY)** : As one of the most iconic ETFs, SPY continues to thrive on the stability and consistent performance of S&P 500 companies, providing exceptional diversification and liquidity.

---

[1] https://markets.businessinsider.com/news/etf/cathie-wood-s-ark-invest-lost-more-than-14b-in-wealth-over-past-decade-report-1033037251

[2] https://www.justetf.com/en/market-overview/the-worst-etfs.html

3. **Vanguard Total Stock Market ETF (VTI)** : Providing exposure to the entire US stock market, VTI has demonstrated strong performance with a full replication approach and low management fees, attracting many investors.

***

By studying the successes and failures of ETFs, we better understand the opportunities and dangers they present. The lessons learned from these historical experiences are essential to carefully and effectively navigating the complex world of Exchange Traded Funds. Whether you are a novice or seasoned investor, this in-depth understanding is crucial to maximizing your gains while minimizing risks.

1.3. Differences between ETFs and other funds (mutual, closed, etc.)

Here is a subject of great importance in the modern financial world: Exchange Traded Funds, more commonly called ETFs. These financial instruments, which combine the benefits of stocks and mutual funds, have transformed the way we invest. Our objective here is to understand these tools, explore their mechanisms, and evaluate their place in the current financial landscape. With a positive and open approach, we will seek the truth without taking sides or arguing about the dangers or opportunities they represent.

To fully understand what an ETF is, it is crucial to compare it with other types of investment funds, such as mutual funds and closed-end funds. These distinctions will allow us to fully appreciate the unique characteristics of ETFs.

ETFs, dangerous financial instruments?

Mutual Funds

Mutual funds are well-established investment vehicles that pool the money of many investors to purchase a variety of securities, such as stocks, bonds and other assets. These funds are managed by professional portfolio managers who make investment decisions based on the fund's objectives.

One of the main differences between mutual funds and ETFs is how they are traded. Mutual funds are bought and sold at the net asset value (NAV) price which is determined at the end of each trading day. This means that trades are executed once a day, after the markets close.

Closed Funds

Closed-end funds (CEFs) are similar to mutual funds in that they pool investors' resources to purchase diversified securities. However, there are notable differences. Closed-end funds issue a fixed number of shares when they go public and those shares are then traded on an exchange, like common stock. The market price of a closed-end fund's shares may fluctuate based on supply and demand, often deviating from the net asset value of the underlying assets.

Exchange Traded Funds (ETFs)

ETFs combine elements of mutual funds and closed-end funds. Like mutual funds, they offer diversification and are managed by professionals. However, like closed-end funds, ETFs trade on exchanges throughout the trading day. This allows investors to buy and sell ETF shares at any time during market hours, at prices that fluctuate based on supply and demand.

A distinctive advantage of ETFs is their transparent structure. Most ETFs disclose their holdings daily, allowing investors to know exactly what they are investing in. Additionally, ETFs tend to have lower management fees compared to mutual funds, in part due to their passive structure which often tracks market indexes rather than seeking to beat the market.

***

ETFs, dangerous financial instruments?

In summary, although mutual funds, closed-end funds and ETFs share common objectives of diversification and professional management, their operating mechanisms and trading structures differ significantly. These differences provide investors with a variety of options to meet their specific needs and investment preferences. By exploring these nuances, we can better understand how ETFs can fit into an overall investment strategy and help us navigate the world of financial investing with confidence.

Part I: ETF Fundamentals

2. How ETFs Work

2.1 Structures and Types of ETFs

Let's dive into the fascinating world of ETFs, these modern financial tools which offer a multitude of investment possibilities, like the diversity of content on a streaming platform. Through this exploration, we will discover the different ETF structures, each tailored to specific strategies and objectives, with contemporary cultural references to make the subject more accessible.

Index ETFs: The Great Classic

Like the superhero movies that dominate the box office, index ETFs are the undisputed stars of the ETF world. These funds passively track a benchmark index, such as the S&P 500 or Nasdaq-100, faithfully replicating the performance of these indices. They are appreciated for their simplicity and effectiveness. Investing in an index ETF is a bit like choosing to watch the latest Marvel blockbuster: you know you won't be disappointed, thanks to the solidity and reputation of these products.

Sector ETFs: Specialized Spin-offs

Sector ETFs are comparable to spin-offs of successful series, focused on a particular theme or character. These funds focus on specific sectors such as technology, health or energy. It's like following "Better Call Saul" after loving "Breaking Bad" — a deep dive into a particular field that can offer high returns if the industry prospers.

Actively managed ETFs: Arthouse Film Directors

These ETFs are the equivalent of independent arthouse films, where every decision is carefully made by professional managers seeking to beat the market. Unlike index ETFs that passively track an index, actively managed ETFs use the expertise and research of managers to attempt to achieve superior returns. Think of a Quentin Tarantino film: unpredictable, often brilliant, and requiring an appreciation for the art of active management.

Leveraged ETFs: The Financial Roller Coaster

For thrill-seekers, leveraged ETFs are like a roller coaster at an amusement park. They use debt to amplify the gains (or losses) of a given index. Investing in a leveraged ETF is like watching a horror movie at midnight – thrilling and exciting, but only for those with a high risk tolerance and strong hearts.

Inverse ETFs: The Upside Down of Stranger Things

Finally, inverse ETFs thrive when the market is down, turning market losses into gains for their holders. It's like diving into the upside-down world of "Stranger Things" – a universe where everything is turned upside down. These funds are powerful tools for risk management, helping to protect a portfolio against market declines, but they require a clear understanding of how they work.

***

ETFs offer a diverse range of structures suitable for various investment styles, much like the variety of film and series genres on a streaming platform. Choosing the right type of ETF depends on your financial goals, risk tolerance and investment strategy. Whether you're drawn to the stability of index blockbusters, the intensity of sector thrillers, or the daring of actively managed arthouse films, there's an ETF for every investor. Sit back and get ready to discover the many facets of these fascinating investment tools.

2.2. Creation and Redemption Mechanisms

Let's imagine for a moment that you are a chef in a Michelin-starred restaurant, preparing a complex dish with exquisite ingredients. Similarly,

ETFs, dangerous financial instruments?

ETFs are created and redeemed through a meticulous and sophisticated process, orchestrated by key players in the financial world. Let's dive into this financial kitchen, where precision and expertise are essential.

Creating ETFs: Like Assembling a Tasting Menu

Creating an ETF begins with a process called "in-kind creation," much like assembling the ingredients for a tasting menu. "Authorized Participants" (APs), often large financial institutions, play the role of star chefs. They buy the underlying securities that will make up the ETF, such as stocks or bonds, and package them into what is called a "creation basket."

Imagine the chef carefully preparing the ingredients: each stock or bond is selected and measured precisely, ensuring that the basket accurately reflects the index that the ETF aims to track. Then, this basket is delivered to the ETF provider, who in exchange issues shares of the ETF to the APs. It is as if our chef presented his finalized dish to the restaurant for service, ready for customers to enjoy.

ETF Redemption: Cleaning the Kitchen After Service

Now let's move on to the redemption, which can be compared to the meticulous cleaning of the kitchen after a lively evening. When an investor wants to sell a large quantity of ETF shares, APs step in again. They buy back these shares in exchange for an equivalent basket of underlying securities. It's a bit like the chef picking up the remaining dishes and ingredients, making sure everything is put away and clean for the next service.

This redemption process helps maintain the efficiency of the ETFs, ensuring that the unit price remains close to the net asset value (NAV). If an ETF's price deviates too much from its NAV, APs can step in to arbitrage the difference, much like a maître d' ensuring that each client receives impeccable service, adjusting the details in real time.

Innovation and Technology: The Cuisine of Modern Finance

As in any great kitchen, innovation and technology play a crucial role. ETFs have benefited from significant advances in electronic trading and risk management. Modern trading platforms enable fast and efficient transactions, reducing costs and improving liquidity. It's like using the latest kitchen gadgets to prepare a meal faster and with more precision.

Additionally, sophisticated algorithms and data analytics enable APs and fund managers to monitor markets in real time, thereby optimizing creation and redemption processes. Imagine a chef using a mobile app to monitor the temperature and humidity in their kitchen, ensuring that every dish is prepared in perfect conditions.

***

The creation and redemption mechanisms of ETFs are complex but essential processes, ensuring that these financial products operate smoothly and efficiently. By understanding these mechanisms, we can better appreciate the intricacies of these investment tools, just as a gourmet appreciates each step of preparing a star meal.

As we continue our exploration of ETFs, let's keep in mind that, as with all good cooking, precision, innovation and vigilance are the keys to success. Whether you are a newbie investor or a seasoned veteran, this understanding will allow you to confidently navigate the fascinating world of Exchange Traded Funds.

2.3. Roles of Authorized Participants

Let's go behind the scenes of the financial theater, where a sophisticated ballet orchestrated by Authorized Participants (APs) is played out. If the ETFs are the stars of the stage, the PAs are the invisible directors who ensure that the show goes off without a hitch. Their role is essential in maintaining the liquidity and stability of ETFs, and they deserve a standing ovation for their meticulous work. Let's take a look at their functions.

Market Mechanics: A Professional Job

Authorized Participants are often renowned financial institutions, such as Goldman Sachs or JP Morgan, which act as mechanics of the financial markets. Think of them like the pit crews of Formula 1, ready to step in at any moment to make sure the car (the ETF) is running at full speed. They are responsible for the creation and redemption of ETF shares, acting as intermediaries between the primary and secondary markets.

Creation of ETFs: Financial Alchemy

When there is increased demand for an ETF, APs come in to create new shares. Think of them as modern-day alchemists, turning a basket of stocks or bonds into ETF shares. They do this by purchasing the underlying securities and combining them into a "creation basket." In exchange for this basket, the ETF issuer issues them shares of the ETF, which can then be sold on the market. It's a bit like PAs preparing raw ingredients and transforming them into a refined dish ready to be served to hungry investors.

Redemption of ETFs: Ongoing Maintenance

On the other side of the spectrum, when demand for ETF shares decreases, APs will redeem the shares. They take ETF shares from the market and exchange them for the underlying securities. This is essential to maintain the balance between the ETF price and the net asset value (NAV). Imagine a technical maintenance team that ensures the cogs of the machine run smoothly, constantly adjusting parts for optimal performance.

Arbitration: The Guardians of the Balance

PAs also play a crucial role in refereeing. Suppose the price of an ETF deviates from its NAV. APs intervene to exploit these price differences, buying ETF shares when they are undervalued or selling when they are overvalued, while carrying out the corresponding creation or redemption operations. It's a bit like the traders in the world of "The Wolf of Wall Street" but with a touch of wisdom and prudence, ensuring that the market remains balanced and efficient.

Technology and Innovation: PA Tools

ETFs, dangerous financial instruments?

In our digital age, APs use advanced technologies to perform their operations with precision and speed. Trading algorithms and electronic platforms play a key role, enabling near-instant trading and effective risk management. Think of these technologies as James Bond's high-tech gadgets, providing APs with the means to navigate the complexities of the modern marketplace with finesse and agility.

***

Authorized Participants are the invisible but essential players in the world of ETFs, ensuring their creation, redemption and arbitrage with unrivaled expertise. Thanks to their work, ETFs remain liquid, balanced and accessible to investors around the world. By understanding the vital role of PAs, we can better appreciate the complexity and effectiveness of these innovative financial instruments.

Let's continue our exploration of ETFs with a new appreciation for these gatekeepers of modern finance, knowing that behind every smooth transaction is a vigilant AP, ready to intervene to maintain market harmony.

3. Advantages of ETFs

3.1 Diversification and Accessibility

Let's imagine for a moment that you are the director of a big-budget film. You have a host of talented actors at your disposal, each bringing their own unique flavor to the final work. Exchange Traded Funds (ETFs) work in much the same way, offering investors unparalleled diversification and accessibility, like a star-studded cast for your financial portfolio.

Diversification: A Star Casting for Your Portfolio

One of the major strengths of ETFs is their ability to offer instant diversification. Investing in an ETF is a bit like buying a ticket to the latest

ETFs, dangerous financial instruments?

Hollywood blockbuster where every scene is full of stars. A single ETF can contain hundreds or even thousands of different securities, spread across various sectors, regions and asset classes. This reduces risk specific to a single company or sector. It's like not putting all your eggs in one basket, but rather in several baskets, each guarded by a team of financial superheroes.

Take the example of the SPDR S&P 500 ETF (SPY), which tracks the S&P 500 index. By purchasing shares of this ETF, you automatically invest in 500 of the largest American companies, from Apple to Microsoft to Amazon. You benefit from the collective performance of these industry giants without having to buy each stock individually. It's like attending a concert where all your favorite artists perform together on stage – an unbeatable experience.

Accessibility: Investment for All

ETFs make investing accessible to everyone, whether you're a seasoned trader or a curious novice. They trade on stock exchanges, just like stocks, offering flexibility that few other financial products can match. You can buy and sell ETF shares throughout the trading day, at prices that fluctuate in real time. It's like having access to a digital library of films and series, available 24 hours a day, 7 days a week.

Another aspect of accessibility is the low cost associated with ETFs. Unlike traditional mutual funds, which can have high management fees, ETFs are generally less expensive to manage. It's a bit like choosing to watch series on Netflix rather than buying DVDs – more convenient and much cheaper. Lower management fees allow investors to keep more of their earnings, thereby improving their net return.

Passive Investing: Binge-Watching Portfolios

One of the philosophies underlying many ETFs is passive investing, where the aim is to replicate the performance of a market index rather than actively attempting to beat it. It's a bit like binge-watching your favorite series – you let the flow of episodes take you, without active intervention on your part. This passive approach can often outperform active management strategies in terms of risk-adjusted returns, while requiring less time and effort on the part of the investor.

***

The advantages of ETFs, in terms of diversification and accessibility, make them essential in the modern world of investment. They provide a simple, efficient and cost-effective way to access a wide range of assets, enabling all investors, whether novice or experienced, to build robust and diversified portfolios. Like a dream cast or a library of streaming content, ETFs provide the variety and flexibility needed to successfully navigate the contemporary financial landscape.

Embark on this adventure with the confidence that you have at your disposal a powerful and versatile tool, ready to support you in every step of your investment journey.

3.2 Transparency and Liquidity

Imagine you are in a state-of-the-art control room, surrounded by walls of screens displaying real-time data. You can see every move, every decision, every fluctuation in your portfolio. This is what Exchange Traded Funds (ETFs) promise in terms of transparency and liquidity, two fundamental pillars that set them apart in the investment world.

Transparency: Netflix for Investors

The transparency of ETFs is comparable to your experience on Netflix. Imagine that, just as you can browse the complete catalog of films and series available, ETFs offer you total visibility of their content. Most ETFs disclose their holdings daily, allowing investors to know exactly what they are investing in at all times. It's a bit like knowing every actor, every director, and every plot before diving into a binge-worthy series.

ETFs, dangerous financial instruments?

Unlike some mutual funds that only reveal their positions every quarter, ETFs are like a window always open to your investments. You can see every stock, every bond, every security in real time, allowing you to make informed decisions. Think of this transparency like a new season of your favorite series: you know exactly what to expect, avoiding unpleasant surprises.

Liquidity: Uber of Financial Markets

Let's move on to liquidity, the other major advantage of ETFs. In the financial world, liquidity is the ability to quickly buy or sell securities without significantly affecting their price. ETFs shine by their ability to be traded throughout the trading day, at prices that reflect the value of the underlying securities in real time. It's a bit like calling an Uber: you press a button and within minutes you're on your way to your destination.

This flexibility allows investors to react instantly to market changes. Whether to seize an opportunity or to avoid a fall, the liquidity of ETFs offers unparalleled freedom. Imagine being at a Taylor Swift concert and being able to change seats at any time to get a better view of the stage – that's what ETF liquidity allows for in the world of investing.

Liquidity Actors: Market Makers

The unsung heroes of this liquidity are the market makers. These financial institutions, a bit like DJs at a wild party, ensure that the music never stops. They constantly provide buy and sell prices for ETF shares, ensuring you can buy or sell whenever you want, at a fair price. Their role is crucial in maintaining the fluidity and efficiency of the markets, ensuring that investors can dance (or trade) without interruption.

***

Transparency and liquidity are two of ETFs' most powerful assets, transforming the investment experience into an adventure that is both clear and flexible. With complete visibility into your holdings and the ability to move quickly in the market, ETFs give you control and responsiveness comparable to the best modern experiences, whether it's video streaming or instant transport services.

As we continue to explore the many benefits of ETFs, remember that like any good series or service application, these financial instruments are designed to give you the best experience possible. Investing in ETFs is like having a financial superpower at your fingertips, allowing you to navigate the dynamic landscape of financial markets with confidence and agility.

3.3 Tax Efficiency

Let's imagine that you are a military strategist planning a campaign, seeking to maximize your gains while minimizing your losses. Tax-efficient ETFs are the financial equivalent of this well-thought-out strategy, allowing you to navigate the tax maze with the grace and skill of a chess champion.

The Advantage of In-Kind Transactions: The Magician's Trick

One of the main tax advantages of ETFs lies in the in-kind creation and redemption mechanism. Imagine a magician who, through sleight of hand, avoids showing his cards while performing wonders. Similarly, when an Authorized Participant (AP) redeems shares of an ETF, they receive a basket of underlying securities, not cash. This allows the ETF to avoid the sale of securities on the market and therefore not to realize taxable capital gains.

It's a bit like being able to move pieces around a chessboard without ever triggering tax traps. By avoiding cash transactions, ETFs minimize tax-incurring events for investors, allowing them to keep more of their gains.

ETFs, dangerous financial instruments?

Distribution of Capital Gains: The "Stealth" Mode

Unlike traditional mutual funds that regularly distribute realized capital gains to investors, ETFs have a more discreet approach, like a secret agent on a stealth mission. Thanks to their unique structure, ETFs often manage to reduce or completely eliminate capital gains distributions. This means that investors are not subject to capital gains taxes until they sell their ETF shares.

Think of James Bond cleverly dodging motion detectors as he infiltrates an enemy base – that's exactly what ETFs do with taxes, navigating without triggering unnecessary tax liabilities.

Loss Carryover: The Tax Superpower

ETFs also offer the ability to carry forward tax losses, which can be a superpower for investors. In the event of realized losses, these can be used to offset future gains, thereby reducing the overall tax payable. It's like having a "get out of jail free" card in a game of Monopoly, ready to be used at the opportune moment to avoid penalties.

This ability to carry forward losses is particularly useful during periods of market volatility, providing additional flexibility for investors to optimize their long-term tax position.

Dividend Efficiency: The Fruits of the Tax Garden

Finally, ETFs can also offer tax efficiency when it comes to dividends. Some ETFs, particularly those that hold international stocks, may benefit from favorable tax treaties that reduce withholding taxes on dividends. It's like growing a garden where every fruit is carefully harvested and optimally taxed, allowing you to enjoy the profits without a heavy tax burden.

***

The tax efficiency of ETFs is a major advantage that sets them apart from other investment vehicles. Thanks to ingenious mechanisms and an optimized structure, ETFs allow investors to maximize their gains while

ETFs, dangerous financial instruments?

minimizing their tax obligations. It's a bit like playing a game of chess while always being one step ahead of your fiscal opponent.

By understanding and taking advantage of these tax benefits, investors can confidently and astutely navigate the complex world of taxes, ensuring that every move contributes to the growth and protection of their wealth. So, get ready to deploy your tax strategies with the precision of a chess master and the finesse of a secret agent, using ETFs as your tools of choice.

Part II: The Risks of ETFs

4. Market Risk

4.1 Market Volatility and Fluctuations

Let's imagine for a moment that you are on the most extreme roller coaster in the world, those of "Six Flags" or "Disneyland". Each climb is followed by a dizzying descent, each turn makes your head spin, and the adrenaline is at its peak. Welcome to the world of volatility and market fluctuations, a playground where ETFs (Exchange Traded Funds) are not spared from sudden and unpredictable movements. Let's explore this chaotic terrain together:

Volatility: The Big Eight of Investments

Volatility is to finance what roller coasters are to amusement parks: exciting for some, terrifying for others. ETFs, like any other form of investment, are subject to the vagaries of the market. When the stock market is hot, ETF prices can skyrocket or fall sharply, reflecting movements in the underlying securities they hold.

Imagine you're a character in a Marvel superhero movie, where every battle could either save the world or spell its doom. Likewise, market volatility can turn a gain into a loss in the blink of an eye. Take the ARK Innovation ETF (ARKK), for example, which has experienced extreme volatility, going from dizzying highs to abysmal lows in no time, much like the Hulk during a tantrum.

Market Fluctuations: Dancing with the Elements

Market fluctuations are like the tides of the ocean, influenced by forces that are often invisible and unpredictable. These movements can be triggered by macroeconomic events, political changes, technological innovations or even tweets from famous influencers. Remember Elon Musk's tweet that caused the price of Dogecoin to jump – a clear demonstration of the power of market fluctuations.

For ETF investors, this means it is crucial to stay informed and understand the underlying factors that may affect their investments. Market fluctuations aren't just numbers on a screen; they represent the heartbeat of the global economy. Each movement is a note in the complex symphony of financial markets.

Managing Volatility: The Strategies of Financial Superheroes

So how do you navigate these rough seas? Just as the Avengers unite to fight a common threat, investors can adopt a variety of strategies to manage volatility. Diversifying your portfolio, for example, is a proven method for mitigating risk. By investing in a variety of ETFs spanning different sectors and regions, you can reduce the impact of extreme fluctuations in a single asset class.

Additionally, using inverse or leveraged ETFs can be a strategy for those looking to profit from short-term market movements. However, these tools are comparable to Tony Stark's high-tech gadgets - powerful, but requiring in-depth understanding and careful management.

Conclusion: Mastering Market Waves

Market volatility and fluctuations are an integral part of investing in ETFs. As savvy investors, understanding these dynamics is essential to successfully navigating the financial world. Like a roller coaster, there will be ups and downs, but with proper preparation and a well-thought-out strategy, you can turn this experience into a thrilling journey to financial success.

So, fasten your seat belts, prepare yourself for the twists and turns ahead, and remember that every rise and fall is an opportunity to learn and grow in the roller coaster of financial markets.

4.2 Leverage and Inverse ETFs

Let's enter the captivating but perilous world of leverage and inverse ETFs, financial tools as powerful as magic potions in a fantasy novel. They offer spectacular earning opportunities but also carry significant risks. These instruments are comparable to Batman's sophisticated gadgets: formidable in the right hands, but dangerous without proper understanding.

Leverage: The Double Sword of Damocles

Leveraged ETFs are designed to amplify the returns of underlying indices, often by a factor of two or three. Imagine your standard investment is a classic latte. Leveraged ETFs are the turbocharged double espresso, promising to give you a boost, but with the risk of giving you palpitations if you're not prepared.

How it works is simple: these ETFs use derivatives and debt to multiply the daily gains of the index. For example, a 2x leveraged ETF on the S&P 500 aims to double the daily return of that index. If the S&P 500 gains 1% in a day, the ETF should gain around 2%. But be careful, the same logic applies to losses. A drop of 1% translates into a loss of 2%. It's like playing with the volume turned up on your Spotify playlist: the good song electrifies you, but the bad one deafens you.

Inverse ETFs: The Reverse Force of "Stranger Things"

Inverse ETFs, on the other hand, are the Dark Elements of the investment world, thriving in chaos and decay. These funds are designed to generate positive returns when the underlying indices fall. If the market is down, these ETFs soar. It's a bit like the Upside Down from "Stranger Things" – a parallel world where everything works in reverse.

Let's take a concrete example: an inverse ETF on the Nasdaq-100 aims to gain 1% for every 1% decline in this index. For investors anticipating a market correction, these ETFs can be valuable protection tools. However, they are also double-edged. If the market goes up, these ETFs experience proportional losses. They require constant monitoring and active management, much like monitoring fluctuations in cryptocurrencies after a tweet from Elon Musk.

Hidden Pitfalls: Decay and Risk of Loss

Both types of ETFs present an additional challenge: the phenomenon of "decay" or erosion of time. Due to their daily reset, leveraged ETFs and inverse ETFs do not perfectly track the underlying index over an extended period of time. This divergence can lead to significant losses over the long term, even if the index eventually reaches its intended target. It's a bit like watching a series on Netflix where each episode becomes progressively less coherent – frustrating and potentially disastrous if you don't follow carefully.

Mastering Market Forces

Leveraged ETFs and Inverse ETFs are powerful tools that, used well, can provide unique opportunities in volatile markets. However, their complexity and high risk make them unsuitable for unsophisticated investors. Like any good superhero or strategist, it is crucial to know your weapons, understand their mechanics and use them with caution.

Ultimately, these instruments require rigorous management and a thorough understanding of market dynamics. Used correctly, they can be great allies in your quest for financial gains. But, without adequate preparation, they can become formidable adversaries, ready to devour your investments. Be the master of your financial destiny, not a victim of the whims of the market.

5. Tracking Risk (Tracking Error)

5.1 Tracking Errors and Performance

The world of ETFs is often compared to a complex choreography where each movement must be perfectly synchronized with the music to achieve perfection. However, even the most experienced dancers can miss a step or deviate from the rhythm. This phenomenon, known as "tracking error", represents the divergence between the performance of an ETF and that of its benchmark index. Let's dive into this exciting topic.

Tracking Errors: When the Orchestra Loses Tempo

Tracking errors occur when the ETF fails to exactly replicate the returns of its benchmark. Imagine that you are attending a concert where the orchestra is playing a Beethoven symphony. Each musician must follow the score to the letter. If a violinist decides to play an improvised solo right in the middle of the movement, it creates dissonance. Likewise, factors such as management fees, transaction costs, and market fluctuations can cause deviations between the ETF and its index.

For example, an ETF tracking the S&P 500 Index might underperform the index slightly due to annual management fees. This difference, however small, accumulates over time and can impact investors' returns. It's a bit like streaming "Game of Thrones" with an unstable internet connection - every little interruption can ruin the overall experience.

The Causes of Tracking Errors: A Complex Puzzle

Several factors can contribute to tracking errors, creating a complex puzzle for investors. Management fees are often the obvious culprits. Although ETFs are known for their low costs, these fees still exist and reduce returns. Then there are transaction costs associated with portfolio adjustments, particularly when the ETF must buy or sell securities to stay in line with the index. Think of these costs like additional shipping fees when ordering your favorite sneakers on StockX.

Additionally, dividends not immediately reinvested can also cause tracking errors. When index constituents pay dividends, those amounts must be reinvested in the ETF, which may not happen instantly. This creates a delay, a bit like waiting for the new season of "Stranger Things" to finally be available on Netflix.

Measuring Tracking Errors: Key Indicators

To evaluate how well an ETF tracks its index, investors can use several indicators. The most common is the tracking difference, which measures the difference in returns between the ETF and its index over a given period. Another tool is tracking volatility, which assesses the variability of these tracking differences. These measurements help verify whether the ETF is dancing to the rhythm of its index or whether it is taking creative liberties, like a freestyle dancer in a ballet competition.

Minimizing Tracking Errors: The Art of Discipline

ETF managers strive to minimize tracking errors by optimizing management strategies and using advanced techniques such as sampling, which consists of selecting a representative subset of the securities in the ETF. hint. They can also use derivatives to quickly adjust exposures. It's a bit like a chef using specific spices to faithfully reproduce a traditional recipe with locally available ingredients.

***

Tracking errors are an inevitable challenge in managing ETFs, but with a thorough understanding of their causes and impacts, investors can make more informed decisions. Like a complex choreography or a well-executed series, precisely following a clue requires rigor, precision and a little technical wizardry. By mastering these elements, ETFs can offer performance close to the index, allowing investors to navigate the vast universe of financial markets with confidence.

5.2 Concrete Examples of Significant Tracking Errors

In the world of ETFs, tracking error is a crucial indicator that can have a significant impact on investor returns. This phenomenon represents the divergence between the performance of an ETF and that of its benchmark index. Let's look at some real-world examples of tracking errors to understand how and why they happen, with a touch of cultural relevance for our financial audience.

1. SPDR Barclays Capital High Yield Bond ETF (JNK)

The SPDR Barclays Capital High Yield Bond ETF, known by the symbol JNK, is a classic example of an ETF suffering from high tracking error. This ETF tracks the Barclays Capital High Yield Very Liquid Index, which is comprised of high-yield bonds. However, due to high transaction costs and low liquidity of the underlying bonds, tracking error can be notable. The very nature of high-yield bonds, often volatile and less liquid, makes it difficult to accurately replicate the index. This situation is comparable to trying to capture a live concert performance on a recording – key elements may be lost along the way (Nasdaq)[3].

2. United States Oil Fund (USO)

The United States Oil Fund (USO) is an ETF designed to track movements in the price of crude oil. However, USO has experienced significant divergences from actual oil prices, particularly during periods of high market volatility. The rolling costs of futures contracts and the frequent adjustments required to track oil prices have led to significant tracking errors. It's a bit like following the adventures of "The Mandalorian" but with episodes that don't always come in the right order – the end result can be confusing (Investopedia)[4].

3. iShares MSCI Emerging Markets ETF (EEM)

The iShares MSCI Emerging Markets ETF (EEM) also exhibited notable tracking errors, primarily due to high transaction costs and liquidity challenges in emerging markets. Local currency fluctuations and regulatory differences between countries contribute to increasing costs and creating gaps between the ETF and its benchmark. It's similar to trying to follow an international recipe with local ingredients – the

---

[3] https://www.nasdaq.com/articles/etfs-high-tracking-error-2012-10-18

[4] https://www.investopedia.com/articles/exchangetradedfunds/09/tracking-error-etf-funds.asp

subtleties of flavors can be lost in translation (Investopedia)⁵ (ETF Stream)⁶.

4. Vanguard REIT ETF (VNQ)

The Vanguard REIT ETF (VNQ), which tracks the MSCI US REIT Index, has also shown tracking errors due to the nature of real estate assets. Property management costs, liquidity variations and frequent adjustments to reflect new property acquisitions and sales contribute to discrepancies. Imagine watching "Selling Sunset" and trying to predict home prices in real time – unexpected fluctuations can make the task complex and inaccurate (ETF Stream).

***

Tracking errors are a pervasive challenge for ETF managers, potentially affecting investor returns. Transaction costs, liquidity of underlying assets, and market fluctuations are all factors that can contribute to these divergences. By understanding these real-world examples, investors can better assess risks and make more informed decisions in their quest for optimized returns. As always, constant vigilance and a good understanding of tracking mechanisms are essential to navigating the complex world of ETFs.

6. Liquidity Risk

6.1 Liquidity Issues in Volatile Markets

Navigating the stormy waters of the financial markets is a bit like trying to cross the Atlantic in a storm. Exchange Traded Funds (ETFs), while generally robust and flexible, are not immune to liquidity issues, especially

---

[5] https://www.investopedia.com/terms/t/trackingerror.asp

[6] https://www.etfstream.com/education/essentials/etfs-tracking-error-vs-tracking-difference

when markets become volatile. Let's understand these challenges together.

Liquidity Challenges: The Roller Coaster Show

Liquidity problems arise when trading volumes become insufficient to absorb buy or sell orders without causing significant price movements. In volatile market times, investors often behave like hysterical fans when a new Beyoncé album comes out: everyone wants to buy or sell at the same time, creating traffic jams and price distortions.

A prominent example is the flash crash of 2010, where sudden massive sell-offs caused stock prices to fall sharply, also affecting ETFs. During these moments of panic, spreads between bid and ask prices widen, and trades become more expensive and less predictable. It's a bit like trying to buy tickets to a Taylor Swift concert – the sudden demand far exceeds the supply, creating monumental chaos (Investopedia)[7].

Concrete Cases: The Stress of ETFs during Crises

During the COVID-19 crisis in March 2020, the financial world experienced an episode worthy of "Stranger Things". Markets plunged into the unknown, and ETFs were not spared. Some high yield bond ETFs, such as the iShares iBoxx $ High Yield Corporate Bond ETF (HYG), have seen their prices diverge significantly from net asset value (NAV). The investors, like the characters in the series, found themselves in a situation where the familiar terrain suddenly became terrifying and unpredictable (ETF Stream)[8].

Additionally, ETFs exposed to specific sectors, such as renewable energy or emerging technologies, may suffer from liquidity problems that are exacerbated during periods of stress. The Global

---

[7] https://www.investopedia.com/articles/exchangetradedfunds/09/tracking-error-etf-funds.asp

[8] https://www.etfstream.com/education/essentials/etfs-tracking-error-vs-tracking-difference

ETFs, dangerous financial instruments?

Liquidity Solutions: The Silent Superheroes

Fortunately, financial markets have their own Avengers to combat these liquidity challenges. Market makers and Authorized Participants (APs) play a crucial role in maintaining balance and smooth trading. By providing consistent buying and selling prices, these players facilitate trading even in turbulent times. It's as if Iron Man and Captain America are working behind the scenes to ensure the chaos is brought under control and order is restored.

Regulators, such as the SEC in the United States, have also put safeguards in place to protect investors. Mechanisms like circuit breakers can temporarily suspend trading when prices move too quickly, allowing markets to catch their breath. It's a bit like a well-deserved break from a binge-worthy Netflix series – it gives you time to digest the action before diving back into the plot.

***

Liquidity issues in volatile markets are a constant challenge for ETFs, testing their robustness and flexibility. Understanding these dynamics and how market navigators (market makers, regulators) work to mitigate these risks can help investors make more informed decisions. Like any good series or movie, knowing what goes on behind the scenes adds a depth of understanding and security to your investing experience.

As you continue your financial journey, remember that even in the most chaotic times, there are heroes and systems in place to maintain stability and confidence in the market.

7. Counterparty Risk

7.1 Implications of Trading in Derivatives and Synthetic Products

In the world of ETFs, counterparty risk is a component as intriguing as the plots of the series "Game of Thrones". Complex and potentially devastating, it can turn a safe investment into a perilous adventure. Let's dive into the depths of this risk, exploring the implications of derivatives trading and synthetic products.

Derivatives and Synthetic Products: The Magic Potions of Finance

Derivatives and synthetics in ETFs are like magic potions in a fantasy novel: they offer incredible powers, but at a price. Synthetic ETFs use swap contracts to track the performance of an index. Rather than directly holding the underlying assets, these ETFs enter into agreements with financial counterparties, often banks, who agree to pay the performance of the index in exchange for a set of assets or a amount of money.

Imagine that you have signed a pact with a sorcerer who promises to double your wealth every year. It's fantastic, until the wizard mysteriously disappears one night, taking your hopes and your money. In the case of ETFs, if the counterparty defaults – for example, if the bank becomes insolvent – the ETF and its investors can suffer significant losses. It's a bit like "Harry Potter," where magical items can cause unexpected problems if they fall into the wrong hands.

Hidden Risks: When the Magic Works (or Not)

Counterparty risk is not always apparent, and therein lies the danger. Investors may not be aware of the underlying swap agreements that support the returns of their synthetic ETF. For example, during the 2008 financial crisis, many derivatives suddenly revealed their vulnerability when banks, once considered infallible, found themselves on the brink of bankruptcy. This situation has revealed how hidden but potentially destructive counterparty risk can be.

Synthetic ETFs can offer benefits such as better liquidity and more accurate replication of complex indices. However, these benefits must be weighed against the possibility that the counterparty will not be able to honor its obligations. It's like buying a great replica of a rare collectible – it seems perfect until you discover it's falling apart in the rain.

Concrete example: Le Cas de Lyxor ETF

A telling example is that of Lyxor ETF, a subsidiary of Société Générale. Lyxor uses swaps to replicate the performance of its target indices. Although this strategy allows for precise and often less costly replication, it also exposes investors to Société Générale's counterparty risk. If the bank encounters financial difficulties, Lyxor ETF investors could suffer the consequences. It is a reminder that even respected institutions are not immune to economic and financial turbulence ([Fidelity Investments](#))[9].

Mitigation Strategies: Protective Shields

To protect against counterparty risk, ETF managers and investors can adopt several strategies. First, diversifying counterparties so as not to depend on a single entity is crucial. It's like making sure your army in "The Witcher" doesn't rely on a single hero but a coalition of sturdy warriors.

Additionally, some ETFs use collateral to secure swap agreements. This means that assets of equivalent value are held as collateral, thereby reducing risk in the event of counterparty default. This practice is similar to having a magical backup plan – a powerful item kept safe in case things go wrong.

***

Counterparty risk in synthetic ETFs and derivatives trading is a critical aspect that every investor must understand. Although these instruments can offer attractive return opportunities and accurate replication of

---

[9] https://www.fidelity.com/learning-center/investment-products/etf/fixed-income-etfs-liquidity

indices, they carry hidden risks that can have serious consequences. By keeping real-world examples and mitigation strategies in mind, investors can navigate this complex terrain with adequate preparation, much like well-equipped heroes in a fantasy epic.

7.2 Case Study on Counterparty Risks

The world of ETFs is not without its perils, and among these, counterparty risk is one of the most insidious. This risk arises when the other party in a financial agreement, usually a bank or financial institution, cannot honor its obligations. Let's look at some real-world case studies to understand how this risk can manifest itself and what the implications are for investors.

The Case of Lehman Brothers and Synthetic ETFs

The emblematic case of Lehman Brothers in 2008 is often cited to illustrate counterparty risk. Before its bankruptcy, Lehman Brothers was a counterparty in many swap agreements used by synthetic ETFs to track the performance of indices. When the bank failed, the affected ETFs were left with illiquid or worthless assets in place of expected returns. This case highlighted the vulnerability of synthetic ETFs to the failure of their financial counterparties (Funds Europe) (Funds Europe)[10].

db x-trackers and Counterparty Risk Management

db x-trackers, a series of ETFs managed by Deutsche Bank, has also faced concerns about counterparty risk. To mitigate this risk, Deutsche Bank introduced a fully collateralized NAV (net asset value) structure, where assets are held in a separate secure account. This approach ensures that even in the event of counterparty default, investors can recover their funds through collateralized assets. This strategy allowed db x-trackers to

---

[10] https://www.funds-europe.com/etfs-counterparty-risk/

strengthen investor confidence in times of financial turbulence (Morningstar) (Morningstar)[11].

The Bond Market and Synthetic ETFs

Another example is synthetic bond ETFs, which use swaps to replicate the performance of bond indices. These ETFs are particularly exposed to counterparty risk due to the illiquid nature of the underlying bonds. During periods of stress, such as the 2008 financial crisis or the COVID-19 pandemic, liquidity in bond markets often dries up, making swaps difficult to manage. This situation can result in significant deviations between the value of the ETF and its benchmark, exacerbating counterparty risk for investors (ECB) (European Central Bank)[12].

***

Counterparty risks in ETFs, particularly those using derivatives and synthetic products, are a complex and potentially dangerous reality. The examples of Lehman Brothers and db x-trackers show that although steps can be taken to mitigate these risks, they can never be entirely eliminated. Investors must be vigilant and well informed, scrutinizing the underlying mechanisms of ETFs and the financial strength of their counterparties. By keeping these lessons in mind, they can more carefully navigate the complex world of synthetic ETFs and derivatives.

---

[11] https://www.morningstar.co.uk/uk/news/68769/Understanding-Counterparty-Risk-in-ETPs.aspx

[12] https://www.ecb.europa.eu/press/financial-stability-publications/fsr/special/html/ecb.fsrart201811_3.en.html

8. Regulatory Risk

8.1 Current Regulatory Framework and its Limits

In the world of ETFs, regulatory risk is as unpredictable as the twists and turns of "Stranger Things." This risk arises from changes in laws and regulations that may impact the way ETFs are managed, marketed and traded. Let's look at the current regulatory framework, its limitations and some implications for investors.

The Current Regulatory Framework: A Changing Ecosystem

The regulatory framework for ETFs is a true global patchwork, with significant variations depending on jurisdiction. In the United States, ETFs are primarily regulated by the Securities and Exchange Commission (SEC) under the Investment Company Act of 1940. In Europe, ETFs must comply with the UCITS (Undertakings for Collective Investment in Transferable Securities) guidelines, which impose strict rules on asset diversification and investment transparency.

In the United States, SEC Rule 6c-11, nicknamed "ETF Rule", adopted in 2019, aims to standardize and simplify the process of launching and managing ETFs. This rule allows managers to launch new ETFs without seeking specific exemptions, accelerating innovation and competition in the market. However, the speed with which new products can be introduced raises questions about the rigor of initial controls, much like seasons of "The Mandalorian" that arrive quickly but with sometimes rushed story arcs (European Central Bank) (Funds Europe).

The Limits of Regulation: When the Frame is Too Narrow

Despite these efforts, the current regulatory framework has notable limitations. For example, existing regulations are struggling to keep pace with financial innovations, particularly in terms of complex derivatives and alternative investment strategies. Synthetic ETFs, which use swaps to track indexes, raise particular concerns about transparency and counterparty risk, often compared to the unanticipated scenes in "Black Mirror" that leave viewers perplexed and worried.

In addition, regulations are not always harmonized on a global scale. An ETF that complies with UCITS rules in Europe may not meet SEC requirements in the United States, creating complications for managers seeking to operate in multiple markets. It's a bit like trying to distribute a television series globally while respecting local cultural sensitivities – a complex and sometimes contradictory task.

Implications for Investors: Navigating a Maze

For investors, these regulations and their limits mean that increased vigilance is necessary. For example, during the 2008 financial crisis, regulatory gaps exacerbated the liquidity crisis, severely affecting ETFs and exposing weaknesses in the supervisory framework at the time. Investors must understand not only the underlying assets of their ETFs, but also the specific regulations that govern them.

Regulators have since strengthened transparency requirements, but risks persist. For example, ETFs involved in securities lending add a layer of complexity and risk, often poorly understood by investors. This loan can generate additional income, but it also exposes investors to additional risks, particularly in the event of counterparty default. It's a bit like in "Money Heist" where every brilliant plan carries a huge risk that everything will go wrong (Morningstar)[13].

***

The regulatory framework for ETFs is essential for their proper functioning and the protection of investors, but it is not without flaws. Regulations must evolve quickly to keep pace with financial innovations, while ensuring adequate protection against market, liquidity and counterparty risks. Investors must remain informed and critical, like a savvy audience closely following a thriller series, to successfully navigate this complex and ever-changing landscape.

---

[13] https://www.morningstar.co.uk/uk/news/68769/Understanding-Counterparty-Risk-in-ETPs.aspx

8.2 Regulatory Uncertainties and Potential Impacts

Regulatory uncertainties in the world of ETFs are like the unpredictable release of a new season of "Black Mirror": they can upend expectations and lead to unexpected consequences for investors. These uncertainties can arise from various sources, such as changes in government policy, new financial regulations, or even judicial decisions. Let us analyze these uncertainties and their potential impacts.

Regulatory Reforms: A Slippery Slope

Financial regulations are constantly evolving, and what is true today may be obsolete tomorrow. For example, the Securities and Exchange Commission (SEC) in the United States recently strengthened rules on transparency and risk management for ETFs. These changes are intended to protect investors, but they can also make life more difficult for fund managers, who must continually adapt their strategies to remain compliant. It's a bit like when Netflix suddenly changes the interface of its platform – it can improve the user experience, but it takes time to adapt to find your feet (Funds Europe).

The Risks of Legal Conflicts: Epic Battles

Regulatory uncertainties can also arise from legal battles. A famous case is that of the USO (United States Oil Fund) oil ETF, which faced difficulties due to extreme fluctuations in the oil market in 2020. Regulators had to intervene to limit positions in futures contracts, leading to repercussions on the functioning of the ETF. These interventions have generated great uncertainty for investors, comparable to the season-ending cliffhangers of "Game of Thrones" – no one really knows what will happen next (Morningstar).

The Impacts of Government Policies: Waves of Change

Government policies can also introduce uncertainties. For example, discussions around the taxation of financial transactions may affect the costs associated with investing in ETFs. If a new tax is imposed, it could reduce the attractiveness of ETFs for some investors. It's like a government deciding to tax memes – a small policy change could have a disproportionate impact on a large community of users.

International Regulations: A Complex Dance

ETF managers operating internationally must navigate a maze of different regulations. UCITS guidelines in Europe impose strict requirements, but these regulations may not be aligned with those of the SEC in the United States. This complicates managing global financial products, much like trying to coordinate a flash mob across multiple time zones – it requires careful planning and extraordinary flexibility.

Anticipate the Unpredictable

Regulatory uncertainties are an inevitable part of investing in ETFs. For investors, it is crucial to stay informed and vigilant regarding potential changes in the regulatory landscape. Like any good thriller series, twists and turns can happen at any time, and it's essential to be ready to adapt. By staying abreast of regulatory developments and understanding their implications, investors can navigate this constantly evolving world with greater confidence.

Part III: Case Study and Analyzes

9. ETFs and Cryptocurrencies

9.1 Analysis of Crypto ETFs: Opportunities and Dangers

Crypto ETFs, investment products combining the growing popularity of cryptocurrencies with the accessible structure of ETFs, present both fascinating opportunities and significant risks. Let's dive into the analysis of these modern financial instruments by exploring their pros and cons.

Opportunities: Merging the Best of Both Worlds

Crypto ETFs allow investors to gain exposure to cryptocurrencies without having to directly manage digital assets, which are often perceived as complex and risky. Take for example the ProShares Bitcoin Strategy ETF (BITO), the first Bitcoin futures-based ETF approved in the United States. Since its launch, BITO has attracted an impressive trading volume, reaching 24 million daily trades on average and assets under management of $3.2 billion. It offers investors exposure to Bitcoin without the hassle of digital wallet security (crypto.news)[14] (Investopedia)[15].

Similarly, BlackRock's iShares Bitcoin Trust (IBIT), launching in 2024, has quickly accumulated $14.8 billion in assets under management. It has been able to attract traditional investors thanks to its reliable structure and its management by one of the most respected financial institutions in the world. IBIT makes it easy to invest in Bitcoin through conventional

---

[14] https://crypto.news/best-crypto-etf/

[15] https://www.investopedia.com/pros-and-cons-of-crypto-etfs-8362499

ETFs, dangerous financial instruments?

brokerage accounts, marrying the appeal of cryptocurrencies with the perceived security of traditional investments (crypto.news)[16] (Blockworks)[17].

Dangers: A Perilous Crossing

However, crypto ETFs are not without risks. Extreme price fluctuations of cryptocurrencies are a major challenge. For example, the Grayscale Bitcoin Trust (GBTC) has shown exceptional performance, but its journey is fraught with volatility. In 2023, GBTC recorded a return of 78.51% for the year, but this impressive performance is often accompanied by equally spectacular periods of decline, reminiscent of the most extreme roller coaster (crypto.news) (Blockworks)[18].

Futures-based ETFs, like BITO, also present additional complexities. These products do not hold cryptocurrencies directly but futures contracts, which may result in price discrepancies and additional costs related to rolling contracts. The very structure of futures contracts can lead to lower returns compared to owning the underlying assets directly, especially during periods of high volatility.

Additionally, regulations remain a minefield for crypto ETFs. Recent approvals by the SEC, while encouraging, do not eliminate the risks associated with unregulated cryptocurrency markets. Bankruptcies of platforms like FTX and Voyager Digital have exposed the sector's vulnerabilities, prompting regulators to step up oversight and impose stricter safeguards (Investopedia).

A Delicate Balance

Crypto ETFs represent an exciting advancement in the world of investing, providing opportunities for exposure to cryptocurrencies without the complexities of directly managing digital assets. However, they require a

---

[16] https://crypto.news/best-crypto-etf/

[17] https://blockworks.co/news/crypto-etfs-2024-outlook

[18] https://blockworks.co/news/crypto-etfs-stocks-2023-performance

clear understanding of the inherent risks, including price volatility, futures challenges and regulatory uncertainties.

For savvy investors, crypto ETFs can be a valuable addition to a diversified portfolio, provided they navigate carefully and stay informed of market developments and regulations. As in any good episode of "Black Mirror," the key lies in anticipation and preparation for the unexpected in the digital world.

9.2 Specific cases: Bitcoin and Ethereum ETFs

Bitcoin and Ethereum ETFs have become increasingly popular financial instruments, providing exposure to cryptocurrencies without the complexities of directly managing digital assets. However, they present unique opportunities and risks that merit in-depth analysis.

Bitcoin ETFs: Opportunities and Challenges

The launch of the ProShares Bitcoin Strategy ETF (BITO) in October 2021 marked a significant milestone, becoming the first Bitcoin futures-based ETF approved by the SEC. BITO has seen impressive trading volume since its debut, reaching 24 million daily trades on average. This popularity reflects investors' appetite for products that allow exposure to Bitcoin without having to directly manage digital wallets and associated security issues.

However, futures-based ETFs, like BITO, present challenges. Their returns may diverge from the actual performance of Bitcoin due to futures rolling costs and price differentials. These divergences can become particularly pronounced during periods of high market volatility, making ETF returns potentially lower than those of directly holding Bitcoin.

Ethereum ETFs: A New Wave of Opportunities

The recent approval of ETFs based on Ethereum futures contracts by the SEC opens new possibilities. In October 2023, several Ethereum ETFs were approved, following in the footsteps of the Grayscale Ethereum Trust which is seeking to convert into an Ethereum ETF spot. These products allow investors to participate in the growth of Ethereum, known for its wide range of applications beyond cryptocurrencies, including in the areas of smart contracts and decentralized applications (dApps).

A notable case study is the Valkyrie Bitcoin and Ether Strategy ETF (BTF), which combines the two cryptos and has returned over 90% over the past 12 months, demonstrating the potential of these instruments in a diversified portfolio. However, similar to Bitcoin ETFs, futures-based Ethereum ETFs may also suffer from performance divergence and increased volatility (ThinkAdvisor)[19] (ETF.com)[20] (Blockchain)[21].

Innovation and Regulatory Challenges

The launch of the first spot Bitcoin ETF in Europe, aligned with ESG principles, is another significant innovation. In August 2023, Jacobi Asset Management introduced a Bitcoin ETF on Euronext Amsterdam, with the ambitious goal of meeting environmental criteria by using renewable energy certificates to offset the carbon footprint of Bitcoin held. This approach reflects a growing trend to integrate environmental considerations into financial products linked to cryptocurrencies.

However, regulatory challenges persist. Increased scrutiny from regulators and potential changes in regulations may affect the viability and attractiveness of these products. Investors must remain vigilant in the face of developments in the regulatory framework and the potential impacts on their investments (Zumo.tech)[22].

***

---

[19] https://www.thinkadvisor.com/2023/10/17/ethereum-etfs-are-here-spot-bitcoin-next/

[20] https://www.etf.com/sections/news/ethereum-etf-decision-recalls-spot-bitcoin-launch

[21] https://blockchain.bakermckenzie.com/2023/10/03/an-update-on-the-quest-for-sec-approval-of-spot-bitcoin-etfs/

[22] https://www.zumo.tech/zumo-and-the-future-of-esg-aligned-digital-assets-a-case-study-on-europes-first-decarbonised-spot-bitcoin-etf/

ETFs, dangerous financial instruments?

Bitcoin and Ethereum ETFs offer unique opportunities to diversify a portfolio and access cryptocurrencies in a more structured and regulated manner. However, they also carry specific risks, notably in terms of volatility, rolling costs and regulatory challenges. A thorough understanding of these factors is essential to successfully navigate the world of crypto ETFs. Investors must be prepared to adapt to changing market dynamics and evolving regulations to maximize benefits while minimizing risks.

10. Catastrophe ETF: Case Studies

10.1 Detailed analysis of failed ETFs

ETFs, while powerful and popular, are not immune to failure. The reasons for these failures can vary, from tracking errors to liquidity issues, regulatory risks or design flaws. Let's analyze some real-life cases of failed ETFs, illustrating the lessons for investors.

1. VelocityShares Daily Inverse VIX Short-Term ETN (XIV)

One of the most dramatic examples is the case of the VelocityShares Daily Inverse VIX Short-Term ETN (XIV). This product was designed to reverse the performance of the VIX, an index measuring market volatility. In February 2018, a day of extreme volatility caused a massive loss for this ETF, causing its value to drop 96% in a single day. Investors have learned the hard way that volatility-based products can be devastating in times of intense market stress, highlighting the importance of understanding the underlying mechanics of ETFs before investing in them (AnalystPrep)[23] (Investopedia)[24].

---

[23] https://analystprep.com/study-notes/cfa-level-2/describe-types-of-etf-risk/
[24] https://www.investopedia.com/articles/etfs-mutual-funds/061416/biggest-etf-risks.asp

2. Global X Uranium ETF (URA)

The Global X Uranium ETF (URA) suffered from a combination of poor performance of the underlying assets and weak investor demand. URA invested in companies involved in uranium mining and production, a sector that experienced prolonged difficulties following the 2011 Fukushima nuclear disaster. Declining global demand for uranium and increased regulatory pressures have resulted in a sustained decline in the share prices of companies in this sector, rendering URA unable to generate positive returns for its investors (ETF.com)[25].

3. LYXOR ETF Russia (LXRUS)

The LYXOR ETF Russia (LXRUS) is another notable example. This ETF exposed investors to Russian equity markets. Due to international economic sanctions and political instability, Russian assets have suffered from poor performance and increased volatility. In March 2022, following Russia's invasion of Ukraine, this ETF suspended the creation of new shares, making it difficult for investors to exit the market without suffering significant losses (Investopedia).

4. VanEck Vectors Coal ETF (KOL)

The VanEck Vectors Coal ETF (KOL) has been a victim of the global energy transition and declining demand for coal. Global efforts to reduce carbon emissions and promote cleaner energy sources have greatly impacted coal mining companies. The low performance of coal company stocks, combined with increased regulatory pressures, led to the closure of this ETF in 2020, showing how global trends can influence the viability of sector ETFs (ETF.com).

***

ETF failures offer valuable lessons for investors. They emphasize the importance of understanding the products in which one invests, assessing the inherent risks and remaining informed of trends and regulations that may impact these instruments. Whether due to market volatility, low

---

[25] https://www.etf.com/sections/news/tlt-case-stability

demand, or regulatory pressures, each failure tells a story of necessary vigilance and continuous learning to successfully navigate the world of ETFs.

10.2 Lessons Learned from Closures and Substantial Losses

ETF failures provide valuable lessons on potential pitfalls and best practices for navigating the complex world of investing. Here are some crucial lessons learned from ETF shutdowns and substantial losses.

1. Monitor Compliance and Alignment of Objectives

The case of the O'Shares Global Internet Giants ETF (OGIG) is instructive. Despite a promising start, OGIG was shuttered in 2022 due to disappointing performance and a lack of alignment with investor expectations. Lessons learned: Investors should ensure that the ETF's objectives match their own expectations and risk tolerance, and regularly monitor performance against the benchmark for any significant divergence (Brookings)[26] (FSB)[27].

2. Importance of Liquidity

The Reality Shares DIVCON Dividend Defender ETF (DFND) also closed, primarily due to liquidity concerns. DFND failed to attract sufficient investment volume to maintain narrow spreads and efficient trading. The lesson here is clear: liquidity is crucial for ETFs, and investors must evaluate not only the underlying assets but also the daily trading volume

---

[26] https://www.brookings.edu/events/one-year-later-lessons-learned-from-the-march-2023-bank-failures/
[27] https://www.fsb.org/2023/11/fsb-europe-group-discusses-regional-developments-and-lessons-learned-from-march-bank-failures/

to avoid high transaction costs and difficulties exiting the market (FSB) (Kenda Martin)[28].

3. Understanding the Risks Associated with Complex Products

The failure of the UBS ETRACS 2x Leveraged Long Alerian MLP Infrastructure Index ETN (MLPL) highlights the dangers of complex products. MLPL, a leveraged product, suffered massive losses during the 2016 oil price crash, exacerbated by leverage amplifying market movements. Investors should be particularly careful with leveraged products and ensure they fully understand the mechanisms and associated risks (FSB).

4. Impact of Regulations and Market Changes

The Barclays iPath S&P 500 VIX Short-Term Futures ETN (VXX) ran into issues when new regulations were introduced, affecting the structure of the VIX futures market. Regulations can change quickly and have a significant impact on the viability of a product. Investors should stay informed of regulatory developments and understand how they may impact their investments (Brookings)[29].

5. Anticipate Demand and Market Changes

The VanEck Vectors Coal ETF (KOL) closed in 2020, a victim of declining demand for coal and the transition to renewable energy sources. This case shows the importance of anticipating long-term market trends and diversifying investments to protect against sectoral declines. Investing in declining sectors can lead to significant losses if market conditions change drastically (FSB) (Kenda Martin).

***

---

[28] https://kendamartin.com/lessons-learned-this-year-2023/

[29] https://www.brookings.edu/events/one-year-later-lessons-learned-from-the-march-2023-bank-failures/

ETFs, dangerous financial instruments?

ETF failures reveal key lessons for investors. Understanding products, monitoring liquidity, staying informed of regulations, and anticipating market trends are keys to successfully navigating the world of ETFs. By learning from past mistakes, investors can better prepare and avoid the pitfalls that led to the closure of these funds.

Part IV: Strategies and Recommendations

11. Evaluation of ETFs

11.1 Selection criteria for investors

When selecting an ETF, investors should consider several criteria to ensure they choose the products best suited to their needs and investment objectives. Here are some key criteria, enriched with concrete examples.

1. Fund Size (AUM - Assets Under Management)

An ETF must have a minimum amount of assets under management, often considered to be at least 100 million euros or dollars. A larger size generally ensures better liquidity and reduces the risk of fund closure. For example, ETFs like the SPDR S&P 500 ETF Trust (SPY), with over $300 billion in assets under management, provide excellent liquidity and stability, making trading more efficient and less costly (Investopedia)[30].

2. Management Fees (TER - Total Expense Ratio)

Annual management fees play a crucial role in selecting an ETF. Lower fees allow investors to keep more of their returns. For example, the iShares Core S&P 500 ETF (IVV) has a TER of just 0.03%, making it an attractive choice for long-term investors (ETF portfolios made simple | justETF)[31].

---

[30] https://www.investopedia.com/articles/exchangetradedfunds/08/etf-choose-best.asp

[31] https://www.justetf.com/en/academy/make-the-right-etf-selection.html

3. Transaction Volume

Daily trading volume is a good indicator of an ETF's liquidity. High volume means investors can buy and sell shares more easily, with tighter spreads. The Invesco QQQ Trust (QQQ), tracking the Nasdaq-100 Index, is known for its high trading volume, often exceeding several million shares per day, ensuring optimal liquidity (ETF portfolios made simple | justETF)[32].

4. Tracking Difference

The tracking difference measures the difference between the return of the ETF and that of its benchmark index. A good ETF minimizes this difference, reflecting efficient management and low costs. For example, the Vanguard Total Stock Market ETF (VTI) is known for its low tracking difference, ensuring that investors get returns very close to the index it tracks (Schwab Brokerage)[33].

5. Replication Method

The method of replicating an ETF can be physical (purchase of the underlying assets) or synthetic (use of swaps). Physically replicating ETFs, such as the Vanguard FTSE Developed Markets ETF (VEA), are often preferred for their transparency and lower counterparty risk. However, some investors may find synthetic ETFs advantageous for tracking indices that are more difficult to physically replicate (ETF portfolios made simple | justETF) (ETF portfolios made simple | justETF).

6. Distribution Policy

The dividend distribution policy is also a criterion to consider. ETFs can be distribution (dividends paid to investors) or accumulation (dividends reinvested). Investors looking for regular income may prefer distribution ETFs, such as the SPDR S&P Dividend ETF (SDY), while those aiming for capital growth may opt for accumulation ETFs (Schwab Brokerage).

7. Exposition et Diversification

---

[32] https://www.justetf.com/en/academy/how-to-choose-a-global-etf.html

[33] https://www.schwabassetmanagement.com/content/how-to-evaluate-etfs

An ETF's geographic and sector exposure is crucial for diversification. An ETF like the iShares MSCI Emerging Markets ETF (EEM) provides diversified exposure to emerging markets, reducing country or sector-specific risks. Evaluating the underlying index and its constituents is essential to ensure that the ETF meets the investor's diversification objectives (Investopedia).

***

Selecting an ETF requires an in-depth analysis of several criteria to ensure that it meets the specific needs of investors. By evaluating factors such as fund size, management fees, trading volume, tracking difference, replication method, distribution policy and exposure, investors can make more informed choices and optimize their portfolios to maximize returns while minimizing risks.

11.2 Tools and resources for evaluating ETFs

To navigate the vast world of Exchange-Traded Funds (ETFs), it is essential to have the right tools and resources. Here are some proven platforms and methods that can help you accurately evaluate and compare ETFs.

1. ETF.com

ETF.com is a go-to resource for investors. The site offers a wealth of tools, including detailed analyses, ETF comparisons and fund feeds. Investors can use ETF.com's screener to filter ETFs based on specific criteria such as performance, management fees and trading volume. It's like having a personal financial advisor just a click away, except they don't charge you exorbitant fees every time you ask a question.

2. Morningstar

Morningstar is known for its comprehensive reviews and star ratings, which make it easy to compare ETFs. Their analysis covers aspects such as historical performance, fees, liquidity and risk management. With Morningstar, you can track the performance of ETFs like a fan follows the statistics of their favorite football team – except here, it's your money on the line, not a trophy (StableBread)[34] (Real-Time Financial Data API | Intrinio)[35].

3. YCharts

YCharts offers advanced tools for analyzing ETF performance, comparing fees and assessing risk. The platform also allows data to be visualized in graphs, which is perfect for those who like to see trends rather than just reading numbers. It's a bit like transforming financial data into modern works of art.

4. Investopedia

Investopedia provides detailed guides and educational articles on ETF valuation. Investors can find advice on selecting ETFs, understand expense ratios and tracking differences, and even learn how to avoid common pitfalls. Think of Investopedia as a crash course in finance, but without the boring homework (Investopedia)[36].

5. Vanguard ETF Screener

Vanguard's screener allows investors to filter ETFs based on various criteria, including performance, management fees and asset mix. Vanguard is known for its low costs and high-quality ETFs, making it a great starting point for investors looking for reliability and transparency (StableBread)[37].

6. Schwab ETF Screener

Schwab also offers an ETF screener that allows you to compare products based on performance, fees and liquidity. Schwab's user-friendly interface makes it easy to find the best ETFs based on your specific investment

---

[34] https://stablebread.com/how-to-evaluate-and-compare-etfs/
[35] https://intrinio.com/blog/compare-etfs-process-and-tools-for-etf-comparison
[36] https://www.investopedia.com/articles/etfs-mutual-funds/042616/how-evaluate-etf-performance.asp
[37] https://stablebread.com/how-to-evaluate-and-compare-etfs/

goals. It's like using a dating app to find the perfect ETF – except this one won't ask you weird questions on the first date (Schwab Brokerage).

7. Intrinsic

Intrinio offers sophisticated tools for comparing ETFs, including performance analyzes and detailed risk reports. Their platform is particularly useful for professional investors and portfolio managers looking for advanced data analytics. Intrinio turns ETF research into a Minority Report experience, with data at your fingertips and a futuristic interface (Real-Time Financial Data API | Intrinio).

***

Having the right tools and resources is crucial to evaluating and selecting the best ETFs. Using platforms like ETF.com, Morningstar, YCharts, Investopedia, Vanguard, Schwab and Intrinio, investors can obtain detailed information and compare products to make informed choices. These tools transform the complex process of selecting ETFs into a more manageable and even enjoyable task, allowing investors to navigate the financial world with confidence and competence.

12. Portfolio Management Strategies

12.1 Integration of ETFs into a diversified portfolio

Integrating ETFs into a diversified portfolio is an effective strategy for optimizing performance while minimizing risks. Here are some strategies and tools for integrating ETFs wisely, with a humorous wink and concrete examples.

1. Determine Asset Allocation

Asset allocation is the basis of any portfolio management strategy. It's a bit like following a cake recipe: you need the right proportions of eggs, flour, sugar and milk to obtain a tasty result. A typical allocation might include stocks, bonds, commodities and cash. For example, Ray Dalio's "All Weather" portfolio uses a diversified allocation to withstand all economic conditions, with a split between stocks, bonds and gold (Stock Analysis).

2. Choose the Right ETFs

Once the allocation is defined, the choice of ETFs is crucial. Using a screener like Morningstar allows you to filter ETFs by category, geography and asset type. For example, for global exposure, the iShares MSCI ACWI ETF (ACWI) covers a wide range of international markets, while the Vanguard Total Bond Market ETF (BND) provides comprehensive coverage of the US bond market (Morningstar, Benzinga).

3. Analyze Fees and Performance

Management fees (TER) and past performance are essential criteria. A low-cost ETF like the Schwab U.S. Broad Market ETF (SCHB) with a TER of 0.03% can maximize returns by reducing costs. Additionally, reviewing the historical performance and volatility of the ETF, as ETF.com does, can help evaluate its stability and alignment with investment objectives (Markets.com, Stock Analysis).

4. Consider Liquidity

The liquidity of an ETF ensures that transactions are done easily without additional costs. ETFs with high trading volume, like the SPDR S&P 500 ETF (SPY), offer lower spreads and better market entry and exit. Using platforms like YCharts to check average trading volume is a best practice to ensure liquidity (Benzinga).

5. Check Diversification

For optimal diversification, it is crucial to check that the ETF is not too concentrated in a single sector or region. The Vanguard FTSE All-World ex-US ETF (VEU) is a good example of an ETF offering global diversification outside of the United States, including stocks from developed and emerging countries (Markets.com).

6. Monitor Performance and Rebalance Regularly

Once the ETFs have been selected and integrated into the portfolio, it is important to monitor their performance and rebalance regularly. This means adjusting allocations back to the original proportions defined by the asset allocation strategy. For example, rebalance quarterly or annually to maintain the portfolio's risk-return objective (Benzinga).

***

Integrating ETFs into a diversified portfolio requires careful planning and using the right tools. By following these steps and using trusted resources like Morningstar, ETF.com and YCharts, investors can build a robust and successful portfolio. As in any good culinary strategy, you need the right ingredients and the right proportions to make your investment recipe a success.

12.2 Approaches to limiting the risks associated with ETFs

In the world of investments, ETFs are often seen as versatile and efficient tools. However, as with any investment strategy, it is crucial to manage risks proactively. Here are some approaches to limiting the risks associated with ETFs.

1. Using Collar Strategies

Collar strategies, such as those employed by the Global X Nasdaq 100 Collar 95-110 ETF (QCLR) and the Global allowing limited participation in winnings. These strategies combine the purchase of put options (put options) to limit potential losses and the sale of call options (purchase options) to finance this protection. While this may limit potential gains, it is an effective method for managing market volatility (Global X ETFs)³⁸ (Global X ETFs)³⁹.

2. ETFs Tampons (Buffered ETFs)

Buffer ETFs, like those offered by Halo Investing, offer protection against losses up to a certain threshold (the "buffer"), while limiting gains to a predefined level. For example, if the benchmark index falls 25%, a buffer ETF might only fall 15%, providing some protection against significant market declines. These products use FLEX options to structure desired returns, providing investors with some predictability in volatile market conditions (Halo Journal)⁴⁰.

3. Use of Hedging Options

Hedging options, such as those used by the Cambria Tail Risk ETF (TAIL), are another strategy to mitigate risk. TAIL purchases "out of the money" put options on the S&P 500 index, providing a hedge against significant market declines. By combining these options with U.S. Treasuries, this type of ETF aims to provide income while reducing exposure to market risks. This approach is particularly useful for investors seeking to protect their portfolios against extreme market events (Cambria Funds)⁴¹.

4. Diversification of Assets

Diversification remains a key strategy for risk management. By investing in a diverse range of asset classes, including stocks, bonds, commodities and real estate, investors can reduce the impact of negative performance in a single sector. For example, using ETFs like the iShares MSCI All Country World Index ETF (ACWI) for global exposure and the Vanguard Real Estate

---

[38] https://www.globalxetfs.com/options-collar-strategies-as-a-risk-management-tool/
[39] https://www.globalxetfs.com/risk-management-strategies-for-a-volatile-market-environment/
[40] https://journal.haloinvesting.com/buffered-etfs-gaining-ground-comparing-risk-reduction-strategies/
[41] https://www.cambriafunds.com/tail

ETF (VNQ) for real estate exposure can help balance risk (Global X ETFs) (Global X ETFs).

5. Continuous Monitoring and Rebalancing

Regularly monitoring ETF performance and rebalancing the portfolio is essential to maintaining an asset allocation aligned with risk and return objectives. Markets are constantly evolving, and periodic rebalancing realigns the weights of different asset classes, thus ensuring proactive risk management.

***

Managing ETF risk requires a multi-faceted approach, involving the use of collar strategies, buffer ETFs, hedging options, as well as diversification and ongoing monitoring. By integrating these strategies, investors can navigate volatile markets more confidently and protect their portfolios against significant losses while retaining the potential for reasonable gains.

13. Alternatives to ETFs

13.1 Comparison with traditional funds and other financial products

ETFs (Exchange-Traded Funds) have become popular instruments thanks to their flexibility, transparency and low costs. However, it is essential to understand how they compare to other financial products, including traditional funds such as mutual funds and other alternatives. Let's explore these differences with real-world examples.

1. Management Fees and Costs

ETFs are often praised for their lower management fees compared to mutual funds. According to a NerdWallet study, annual fees for ETFs can be as low as 0.03%, while mutual funds can be as high as 0.60% on average, due to the active management often involved in the latter. These lower ETF fees can significantly increase long-term returns, much like choosing a cheaper but equally entertaining Netflix subscription (NerdWallet, Investopedia).

2. Mode of Negotiation

ETFs trade like stocks on stock markets, which allows for intraday flexibility. Investors can buy or sell ETFs at any time during market hours, at prices that fluctuate throughout the day. On the other hand, mutual funds can only be bought or sold at the end of the trading day, at the price of the net asset value (NAV). It's like being able to order a pizza at any time of the day with ETFs, compared to a single delivery in the evening with mutual funds (Investopedia, TurboTax).

3. Gestion Active vs. Passive

Mutual funds are often actively managed, with fund managers trying to beat the market through stock selections and trading strategies. This active management can result in higher costs and inconsistent performance. ETFs, particularly those that track indices, are generally passively managed, simply seeking to replicate the performance of a benchmark. Statistics show that passive management of ETFs often outperforms active management of mutual funds over the long term, a bit like letting a Roomba automatically clean your house rather than sweeping yourself (NerdWallet, Business Insider).

4. Taxation and Tax Efficiency

ETFs generally offer better tax efficiency than mutual funds. Due to their unique creation and redemption structure, ETF transactions do not trigger taxable capital gains as frequently as mutual funds. Mutual funds must distribute realized capital gains to investors each year, which may result in additional tax liabilities. In other words, investing in ETFs is a bit like choosing a streaming option without pop-up ads, while mutual funds can interrupt you with tax commercials (Investopedia, TurboTax).

5. Diversity of Assets

ETFs, dangerous financial instruments?

ETFs offer a wide range of investment options, including stocks, bonds, commodities and even specific sectors like technology or renewable energy. Mutual funds also offer diversity, but are often limited to more specific strategies. ETFs like the iShares MSCI ACWI ETF allow global exposure in a single transaction, while mutual funds may require multiple purchases to achieve a similar level of diversification (Morningstar, Business Insider).

***

ETFs have distinct advantages over mutual funds and other financial products, including lower costs, greater trading flexibility and greater tax efficiency. However, each type of investment has its own advantages and disadvantages. Investors should evaluate their goals, risk tolerance and preferences to choose the option that suits them best. Understanding these differences can transform your investment strategy, just like choosing between an action movie and a romantic comedy can change your evening.

13.2 Advantages and disadvantages of alternatives

ETFs are popular investment instruments, but they are not the only ones available. Let's compare them to other financial products such as mutual funds, index funds and other alternatives to understand their respective advantages and disadvantages.

1. Mutual Funds

Benefits :

- **Professional Management** : Mutual funds are actively managed by professionals who select securities with a view to outperforming benchmark indices. This can provide an advantage, especially in volatile markets where active management can potentially add value (Investopedia, Wall Street Survivor).

- **Instant Diversification** : By investing in a mutual fund, you immediately gain diversified exposure to a wide range of assets, thereby reducing concentration risk (Investopedia).

Disadvantages:

- **High Fees** : Mutual funds generally have higher management fees, often between 0.5% and 1.5%, due to active management. These fees can erode returns over the long term (NerdWallet).
- **Tax Inefficiency** : Mutual funds can generate taxable capital gains each year, even if the investor has not sold their shares, which can result in additional tax liabilities (Wall Street Survivor).

2. Index Funds (Fonds Indiciel)

Benefits :

- **Low Fees** : Index funds are passively managed and seek to replicate the performance of a specific market index. This results in lower management fees, often around 0.2% (NerdWallet, Finance Strategists).
- **Performance Predictability** : By tracking an index, index funds offer more predictable and consistent performance, which is attractive to investors seeking long-term stability (NerdWallet).

Disadvantages:

- **Limited Return Potential** : Unlike mutual funds, index funds do not seek to beat the market. Their goal is simply to track the benchmark, which can limit potential returns during a bull market (Investopedia).
- **Less Flexibility** : Index funds cannot actively adjust their allocations to take advantage of market opportunities or avoid imminent risks, unlike actively managed mutual funds (Finance Strategists).

3. Hedge Funds

ETFs, dangerous financial instruments?

Benefits :

- **Advanced Strategies** : Hedge funds use a variety of advanced strategies, including short selling, leverage and derivatives, to generate high returns, even in bear markets.
- **High Potential Performance** : With unconventional strategies, hedge funds can offer substantial returns, sometimes outperforming traditional markets.

Disadvantages:

- **Accessibility** : Hedge funds often require high minimum investments, making it difficult for small investors to access.
- **High Fees** : Hedge fund management and performance fees can be exorbitant, with typical structures of 2% management fees and 20% of profits (Investopedia).

***

Each financial product has distinct advantages and disadvantages. ETFs offer low fees and great flexibility, but mutual funds provide active management and immediate diversification. Index funds, with their low fees, are ideal for a long-term passivity strategy, while hedge funds offer sophisticated strategies for potentially high returns, but at a high cost and with barriers to entry. Investors should evaluate their goals, risk tolerance and time horizon to choose the most suitable option.

Part V: Advanced Strategies and Emerging Trends

14. Smart Beta and Factor Investing

14.1 Understanding Smart Beta ETFs

Smart Beta ETFs are a type of investment fund that aim to combine the benefits of passive investing with the potential for higher returns through systematic strategies. Unlike traditional market-cap weighted indices, Smart Beta ETFs follow alternative weighting schemes based on various factors such as volatility, value, size, and momentum. This approach seeks to capture specific risk premia and enhance returns.

The concept of Smart Beta has gained popularity because it addresses some of the limitations of traditional index investing. Traditional indices often have significant exposure to large-cap stocks, potentially leading to concentration risk. Smart Beta strategies aim to mitigate this by diversifying across different factors, thus offering a more balanced risk-return profile.

Example: One notable example is the **iShares Edge MSCI USA Quality Factor ETF (QUAL)**, which focuses on stocks with strong fundamentals, such as high return on equity, stable year-over-year earnings growth, and low financial leverage. This strategy aims to provide investors with exposure to companies that are fundamentally sound and financially healthy.

14.2 How Factor Investing Works

Factor investing involves selecting securities based on attributes that are associated with higher returns. These attributes, or "factors," have been identified through academic research and include:

- **Value:** Investing in stocks that are undervalued relative to their fundamentals.
- **Size:** Focusing on smaller companies with higher growth potential.
- **Momentum:** Investing in stocks that have shown an upward price trend.
- **Quality:** Selecting companies with strong balance sheets and profitability.
- **Volatility:** Targeting stocks with lower volatility to reduce risk.

Factor investing strategies can be implemented through both Smart Beta ETFs and active management. The key idea is that by systematically targeting these factors, investors can potentially achieve higher risk-adjusted returns compared to traditional market-cap weighted indices.

Example: The **Vanguard U.S. Value Factor ETF (VFVA)** focuses on the value factor by investing in U.S. stocks that are considered undervalued based on their price-to-book ratio, price-to-earnings ratio, and other valuation metrics.

14.3 Examples and Performance Analysis

The performance of Smart Beta and factor-based ETFs can vary significantly depending on market conditions and the specific factors targeted. Historically, certain factors like value and momentum have outperformed the broader market over long periods, but they can also underperform during certain market cycles.

Example: The **Invesco S&P 500 Low Volatility ETF (SPLV)** targets the low volatility factor by selecting the least volatile stocks in the S&P 500. During market downturns, this ETF tends to perform better than the overall market due to its focus on lower-risk stocks. Conversely, in strong bull markets, it may underperform as high-risk, high-reward stocks drive the market higher.

A study by MSCI on factor performance from 1975 to 2017 showed that factors like value, size, and momentum provided excess returns over the long term. However, investors should be aware that factors can go through prolonged periods of underperformance, highlighting the importance of diversification across multiple factors.

Conclusion

Smart Beta and factor investing offer sophisticated approaches to ETF investing that blend the benefits of passive strategies with targeted exposure to specific risk factors. By understanding and leveraging these strategies, investors can potentially enhance their portfolios' risk-adjusted returns. However, as with all investment strategies, it is crucial to remain aware of the risks and to diversify appropriately to manage potential periods of underperformance.

15. Environmental, Social, and Governance (ESG) ETFs

15.1 What Are ESG ETFs?

Environmental, Social, and Governance (ESG) ETFs are a type of investment fund that incorporate ESG criteria into their investment process. These criteria are used to evaluate the sustainability and ethical impact of the companies within the ETF's portfolio. The goal is to invest in companies that meet certain standards of environmental stewardship, social responsibility, and corporate governance, thus aligning investments with the values of socially conscious investors.

Environmental Criteria

- Environmental criteria consider how a company performs as a steward of nature. This includes factors like energy use, waste management, pollution, natural resource conservation, and treatment of animals. It also evaluates the environmental risks a company might face and how the company is managing those risks.

Social Criteria

- Social criteria examine how a company manages relationships with employees, suppliers, customers, and the communities where it operates. This includes adherence to labor laws, workplace health and safety, human rights policies, and community engagement. Companies that prioritize diversity and employee welfare typically score higher on the social scale.

Governance Criteria

- Governance criteria involve the internal system of practices, controls, and procedures a company adopts in order to govern itself, make effective decisions, comply with the law, and meet the needs of external stakeholders. This includes issues like board diversity, executive pay, shareholder rights, and transparency.

ESG ETFs aim to provide investors with a way to invest in a diversified portfolio of companies that adhere to these sustainable practices. These funds are becoming increasingly popular as more investors seek to align their portfolios with their personal values and the growing body of evidence suggesting that companies with strong ESG practices can outperform over the long term.

Example: One prominent example of an ESG ETF is the **iShares MSCI KLD 400 Social ETF (DSI)**, which seeks to track the performance of the MSCI KLD 400 Social Index. This index is composed of U.S. companies that have been screened for positive ESG criteria, excluding those involved in activities like alcohol, tobacco, firearms, and gambling.

Growth and Popularity The growth in ESG ETFs has been driven by both institutional and retail investors. According to Morningstar, ESG fund assets reached nearly $2 trillion globally by the end of 2021, reflecting a significant increase in investor interest. This growth is partly due to the increasing recognition that ESG factors can impact financial performance, as well as the rising demand from investors for products that align with their values (Morningstar, BlackRock).

Challenges and Criticisms While ESG ETFs offer numerous benefits, they are not without challenges and criticisms. One major challenge is the lack of standardization in ESG ratings and definitions, which can lead to inconsistencies across different ESG funds. Additionally, some critics argue that ESG criteria can be too subjective and may exclude potentially profitable investments (Bloomberg).

Conclusion

ESG ETFs provide a way for investors to combine financial returns with positive social and environmental impact. By understanding what ESG criteria entail and how they are applied, investors can make informed decisions that align with their values and contribute to a more sustainable future.

References:

1. "What Is ESG Investing?" - Investopedia. Investopedia
2. "The Rise of ESG Investing" - Morningstar. Morningstar
3. "Understanding ESG ETFs" - BlackRock. BlackRock
4. "The Pros and Cons of ESG ETFs" - Bloomberg. Bloomberg

15.2 Growing Popularity and Impact

The popularity of Environmental, Social, and Governance (ESG) ETFs has surged in recent years, reflecting a significant shift in investor preferences and market dynamics. This growth is driven by a combination of increased awareness of sustainability issues, regulatory developments, and a growing body of evidence suggesting that companies with strong ESG practices tend to perform better over the long term.

Increased Investor Demand

Investors are increasingly seeking to align their portfolios with their personal values, leading to a rise in demand for ESG investment options. According to Morningstar, global ESG fund assets nearly doubled in 2020, reaching $2.3 trillion by the end of the year. This trend continued into 2021, with significant inflows into ESG funds, highlighting the growing appetite for sustainable investing (Morningstar).

Retail investors, particularly millennials and Gen Z, are at the forefront of this trend. These younger investors prioritize sustainability and ethical considerations, often favoring companies that demonstrate strong environmental stewardship, social responsibility, and good governance practices. A survey by Morgan Stanley found that 95% of millennials are interested in sustainable investing, underscoring the generational shift in investment priorities (Morgan Stanley).

Institutional Adoption

Institutional investors, including pension funds, endowments, and insurance companies, have also embraced ESG investing. Many institutions are incorporating ESG criteria into their investment processes to manage risks, fulfill fiduciary responsibilities, and respond to stakeholder demands. For instance, BlackRock, the world's largest asset manager, has committed to integrating ESG considerations into its investment strategies, citing the financial materiality of ESG factors (BlackRock).

Regulatory Developments

Regulatory developments worldwide are further propelling the growth of ESG investing. In the European Union, the Sustainable Finance Disclosure Regulation (SFDR) requires asset managers to disclose how they integrate ESG factors into their investment decisions. Similar regulatory initiatives are being considered in other regions, promoting transparency and accountability in ESG investing (European Commission).

Performance and Risk Management

The growing popularity of ESG ETFs is also supported by research indicating that companies with strong ESG practices can deliver superior financial performance. Studies have shown that ESG factors can be material to financial performance, influencing a company's risk profile, operational efficiency, and competitive positioning. For example, companies with strong governance practices tend to have lower incidences of fraud and litigation, while those with robust environmental practices are better positioned to navigate regulatory changes and resource constraints (MSCI).

Impact Investing

Beyond financial returns, ESG ETFs are attracting investors interested in generating positive social and environmental impacts. Impact investing, a subset of ESG investing, aims to produce measurable positive outcomes alongside financial returns. ESG ETFs focusing on renewable energy, clean technology, and social equity are examples of how investors can contribute to societal goals while pursuing their financial objectives (Global Impact Investing Network).

Challenges and Criticisms

Despite their popularity, ESG ETFs face challenges and criticisms. One major challenge is the lack of standardization in ESG metrics and reporting, leading to inconsistencies and greenwashing concerns. Investors may find it difficult to compare ESG performance across different funds and companies. Efforts are underway to address these issues, with organizations like the Task Force on Climate-related Financial Disclosures (TCFD) working to improve ESG reporting standards (TCFD).

Conclusion

The growing popularity and impact of ESG ETFs reflect a broader movement towards sustainable and responsible investing. As investor awareness and regulatory support continue to rise, ESG ETFs are likely to play an increasingly important role in investment portfolios. However, addressing challenges related to standardization and transparency will be crucial to ensuring the integrity and effectiveness of ESG investing.

15.3 Case Studies of Successful ESG ETFs

The success of ESG ETFs can be attributed to their ability to deliver both financial returns and positive social and environmental impacts. Below are detailed case studies of some of the most successful ESG ETFs, illustrating how they have performed and why they have attracted significant investor interest.

1. iShares MSCI KLD 400 Social ETF (DSI)

The iShares MSCI KLD 400 Social ETF (DSI) seeks to track the performance of the MSCI KLD 400 Social Index, which is composed of U.S. companies that have positive ESG characteristics. Since its inception, DSI has been a popular choice for investors looking to align their investments with their values without sacrificing returns.

- **Performance:** Over the past decade, DSI has consistently outperformed the broader market. For instance, as of 2021, it delivered an average annual return of 13.5%, compared to the S&P 500's 12.8% (Morningstar).
- **Impact:** DSI excludes companies involved in controversial activities such as firearms, tobacco, and fossil fuels, thereby ensuring that investors' money supports more sustainable and ethical business practices.

2. SPDR SSGA Gender Diversity Index ETF (SHE)

The SPDR SSGA Gender Diversity Index ETF (SHE) invests in companies with a high representation of women in senior leadership positions. It aims to promote gender diversity in corporate America while offering competitive returns.

- **Performance:** Since its launch in 2016, SHE has provided solid returns, often aligning closely with or outperforming the S&P 500 Index. For example, in 2020, SHE returned 16.3%, compared to the S&P 500's 16.1% (SSGA).
- **Impact:** By focusing on gender diversity, SHE encourages companies to adopt more inclusive practices, which studies have shown can lead to better decision-making and improved financial performance (McKinsey & Company).

3. Vanguard ESG U.S. Stock ETF (ESGV)

The Vanguard ESG U.S. Stock ETF (ESGV) tracks the FTSE US All Cap Choice Index, which excludes companies involved in non-ESG-friendly activities such as adult entertainment, alcohol, tobacco, weapons, fossil fuels, gambling, and nuclear power.

- **Performance:** ESGV has gained popularity for its low expense ratio and strong performance. For instance, from its inception in 2018 through 2021, ESGV delivered an average annual return of 15.2% (Vanguard).
- **Impact:** Vanguard's rigorous screening process ensures that investments are directed towards companies with strong ESG practices, supporting sustainability and ethical business conduct.

4. Invesco Solar ETF (TAN)

The Invesco Solar ETF (TAN) focuses on the global solar energy industry, investing in companies that produce solar power equipment, materials, and services.

- **Performance:** TAN has been one of the best-performing ESG ETFs, particularly benefiting from the global push towards renewable energy. In 2020 alone, TAN returned an impressive 234%, driven by increasing demand for clean energy solutions (Invesco).
- **Impact:** By investing in solar energy, TAN supports the transition to a low-carbon economy, helping to mitigate climate change and reduce reliance on fossil fuels.

5. iShares Global Clean Energy ETF (ICLN)

The iShares Global Clean Energy ETF (ICLN) provides exposure to companies involved in the production of clean energy, including wind, solar, and other renewable sources.

- **Performance:** ICLN has seen substantial growth, particularly in the last few years. From 2019 to 2021, ICLN delivered an average annual return of 34.6% (BlackRock).
- **Impact:** ICLN contributes to environmental sustainability by financing the development and expansion of renewable energy projects worldwide.

Conclusion

These case studies highlight the diverse range of ESG ETFs available and their ability to provide competitive returns while promoting positive environmental and social impacts. The success of these funds demonstrates the growing importance of sustainable investing and the potential for ESG considerations to drive long-term value.

References:

1. "iShares MSCI KLD 400 Social ETF (DSI)" - Morningstar. Morningstar
2. "SPDR SSGA Gender Diversity Index ETF (SHE)" - SSGA. SSGA
3. "Vanguard ESG U.S. Stock ETF (ESGV)" - Vanguard. Vanguard
4. "Invesco Solar ETF (TAN)" - Invesco. Invesco
5. "iShares Global Clean Energy ETF (ICLN)" - BlackRock. BlackRock
6. "Delivering Through Diversity" - McKinsey & Company. McKinsey

16. Thematic Investing with ETFs

Thematic investing with ETFs has gained significant traction as investors seek to capitalize on long-term societal and technological trends. Unlike traditional investment strategies that focus on sectors or regions, thematic investing targets specific themes or trends that are expected to drive growth and innovation in the future. These themes can range from technological advancements, like artificial intelligence and robotics, to societal shifts, such as aging populations or urbanization. Thematic ETFs offer a diversified and efficient way to invest in these transformative trends, allowing investors to align their portfolios with their convictions about the future.

16.1 Introduction to Thematic ETFs

Thematic ETFs are designed to provide exposure to companies and industries that are expected to benefit from specific macroeconomic, technological, or demographic trends. These ETFs do not confine themselves to traditional sector classifications; instead, they select companies based on their involvement in a particular theme or trend.

What Sets Thematic ETFs Apart?

Thematic ETFs stand out because they focus on the potential of future growth drivers rather than current market dynamics. This forward-looking approach allows investors to tap into emerging opportunities that might not yet be reflected in traditional sector or broad-market indices.

Examples of Popular Themes:

1. **Technology and Innovation:**
    - **Global X Robotics & Artificial Intelligence ETF (BOTZ):** This ETF invests in companies involved in the development and production of robotics and artificial intelligence technologies.
    - **ARK Innovation ETF (ARKK):** Managed by ARK Invest, this ETF targets companies that are expected to benefit from disruptive innovation across various sectors, including genomics, automation, energy storage, and financial technology.

2. **Environmental Sustainability:**
    - **iShares Global Clean Energy ETF (ICLN):** This ETF focuses on companies that produce energy from renewable sources such as wind, solar, and hydroelectric power.
    - **Invesco Solar ETF (TAN):** Concentrating on the solar power sector, TAN invests in companies that manufacture solar equipment and provide solar power solutions.
3. **Social Trends:**
    - **Global X Millennials Thematic ETF (MILN):** This ETF targets companies that cater to the preferences and spending habits of the millennial generation, including sectors like technology, social media, and health and wellness.
    - **iShares U.S. Medical Devices ETF (IHI):** Investing in the medical device industry, IHI focuses on companies developing innovative healthcare solutions to address the needs of an aging population.

Advantages of Thematic ETFs:

- **Focused Exposure:** Investors gain targeted exposure to high-growth areas aligned with their investment themes.
- **Diversification:** Although thematic, these ETFs often hold a broad range of companies within the theme, providing some level of diversification.
- **Ease of Access:** Thematic ETFs simplify the process of investing in complex and emerging sectors, offering a cost-effective way to gain exposure.

Risks and Considerations:

- **Concentration Risk:** Thematic ETFs can be heavily weighted towards a small number of sectors or companies, increasing the risk if those areas underperform.
- **Volatility:** Themes based on emerging technologies or trends can be more volatile and subject to rapid changes in market sentiment.

- **Long-term Horizon:** Investors should be prepared for a long-term investment horizon, as thematic plays may take time to materialize fully.

Conclusion

Thematic ETFs offer a compelling way to invest in the future by aligning portfolios with powerful, long-term trends. By understanding the unique characteristics and risks associated with these funds, investors can better position themselves to take advantage of the growth opportunities that thematic investing provides.

References:

1. "What Are Thematic ETFs?" - Investopedia. Investopedia
2. "Thematic Investing with ETFs: A Growing Trend" - Morningstar. Morningstar
3. "ARK Innovation ETF" - ARK Invest. ARK Invest
4. "iShares Global Clean Energy ETF" - BlackRock. BlackRock

16.2 Popular Themes: Technology, Healthcare, Green Energy

Thematic ETFs allow investors to focus on specific sectors or trends that are expected to drive significant growth in the future. Three of the most popular themes in thematic investing are technology, healthcare, and green energy. These sectors are not only at the forefront of innovation but also play a critical role in shaping the global economy and addressing key challenges.

Technology

The technology sector has been a major driver of economic growth and innovation, making it a popular theme for thematic investing. Technology ETFs often focus on companies involved in cutting-edge developments such as artificial intelligence (AI), robotics, cybersecurity, and cloud computing.

- **Global X Robotics & Artificial Intelligence ETF (BOTZ):** This ETF invests in companies involved in the development and production of robotics and AI technologies. BOTZ provides exposure to firms that are leading the way in automation and advanced machine learning.
- **ARK Innovation ETF (ARKK):** Managed by ARK Invest, this ETF targets companies that are expected to benefit from disruptive innovation across various sectors, including AI, robotics, genomic revolution, and next-generation internet.

The tech theme is characterized by high growth potential, but it also comes with higher volatility due to the rapid pace of technological advancements and changes in market dynamics.

Healthcare

The healthcare sector, particularly medical devices and biotechnology, is another prominent theme in thematic investing. The aging global population and increasing focus on innovative medical solutions drive demand in this sector.

- **iShares U.S. Medical Devices ETF (IHI):** This ETF invests in U.S. companies that manufacture medical devices, such as surgical instruments, diagnostic equipment, and prosthetics. The ETF capitalizes on the growing need for advanced medical technologies driven by demographic trends.
- **SPDR S&P Biotech ETF (XBI):** Focusing on the biotechnology sector, XBI includes companies engaged in the research, development, and manufacturing of innovative biological products and therapies.

Investing in healthcare themes provides exposure to a sector that benefits from consistent demand and the potential for breakthroughs in treatments and medical technologies.

Green Energy

Green energy is a rapidly growing theme as the world shifts towards more sustainable and renewable energy sources. Investors are increasingly interested in companies that contribute to environmental sustainability through clean energy production and technologies.

- **iShares Global Clean Energy ETF (ICLN):** This ETF focuses on companies involved in the production of clean energy from renewable sources such as wind, solar, and hydroelectric power. ICLN includes global leaders in the green energy sector, providing diversified exposure to this growing market.
- **Invesco Solar ETF (TAN):** Concentrating on the solar power industry, TAN invests in companies that manufacture solar panels, provide solar power services, and develop solar technologies.

The green energy theme aligns with global efforts to combat climate change and transition to sustainable energy solutions. It offers significant growth potential as governments and corporations commit to reducing carbon footprints and investing in renewable energy infrastructure.

Conclusion

Thematic investing in technology, healthcare, and green energy ETFs allows investors to focus on sectors with strong growth prospects and significant impacts on the future. By targeting these themes, investors can capitalize on transformative trends and potentially achieve higher returns. However, it is crucial to understand the risks associated with thematic investing, including market volatility and sector-specific challenges.

16.3 Risks and Opportunities

Thematic investing with ETFs offers significant opportunities for investors to capitalize on emerging trends and transformative shifts in the global economy. However, this approach also comes with inherent risks that must be carefully managed. Understanding both the risks and opportunities is crucial for making informed investment decisions.

ETFs, dangerous financial instruments?

Opportunities

1. **High Growth Potential**
    - Thematic ETFs often focus on innovative sectors and technologies that have the potential for substantial growth. For instance, the **Global X Robotics & Artificial Intelligence ETF (BOTZ)** targets companies at the forefront of robotics and AI, industries projected to grow exponentially in the coming years (Global X). Similarly, the **iShares Global Clean Energy ETF (ICLN)** capitalizes on the accelerating transition to renewable energy sources, driven by global climate initiatives and increasing adoption of clean technologies (BlackRock).
2. **Alignment with Megatrends**
    - Thematic ETFs allow investors to align their portfolios with long-term megatrends such as digital transformation, demographic shifts, and environmental sustainability. These megatrends are expected to shape the future of the global economy and create new investment opportunities. For example, the **Invesco Solar ETF (TAN)** benefits from the increasing focus on solar energy as a sustainable alternative to fossil fuels (Invesco).
3. **Diversification Benefits**
    - By investing in a specific theme, investors gain exposure to a diverse set of companies within that theme. This diversification can reduce the risk associated with individual stock investments while providing exposure to a broader trend. For instance, the **ARK Innovation ETF (ARKK)** invests across various sectors, including genomics, automation, and energy storage, providing a diversified approach to investing in disruptive innovation (ARK Invest).

Risks

1. **Concentration Risk**
    - Thematic ETFs can be heavily concentrated in a small number of sectors or companies, leading to higher risk if those areas underperform. For example, an ETF focusing

on the biotechnology sector might suffer if regulatory changes negatively impact biotech companies. This concentration risk can lead to significant volatility and potential losses.
2. **Market Sentiment and Volatility**
    - Themes based on emerging technologies or trends can be highly sensitive to market sentiment and short-term fluctuations. Investors in thematic ETFs may experience significant volatility as market perceptions change. For example, the performance of the **SPDR S&P Biotech ETF (XBI)** can be influenced by news related to clinical trial results, regulatory approvals, or changes in healthcare policy (SSGA).
3. **Speculative Nature**
    - Some thematic ETFs may invest in speculative or early-stage companies that have not yet proven their business models. This can lead to higher risk and uncertainty. The **Global X Millennials Thematic ETF (MILN)**, which focuses on companies catering to millennial consumers, includes firms that may still be developing their market presence and profitability (Global X).
4. **Regulatory and Technological Changes**
    - Rapid changes in technology and regulatory environments can impact the performance of thematic ETFs. For instance, advancements in technology could render current innovations obsolete, while regulatory changes could affect the viability of certain business models. Investors must stay informed about the evolving landscape and potential impacts on their thematic investments.

Conclusion

Thematic investing with ETFs offers exciting opportunities to capitalize on transformative trends and high-growth sectors. However, it also comes with risks that require careful consideration and management. By understanding both the potential benefits and the associated risks, investors can make more informed decisions and strategically incorporate thematic ETFs into their portfolios.

17. Sector and Industry ETFs

Investing in sector and industry ETFs allows investors to target specific areas of the economy that they believe will outperform. Unlike broad-market ETFs that spread investments across various sectors, sector and industry ETFs concentrate on particular sectors such as technology, healthcare, or energy. This focused approach enables investors to take advantage of trends and economic cycles that favor specific industries. Sector and industry ETFs provide a way to express market views, manage risk, and capitalize on growth opportunities within defined segments of the market.

17.1 Overview of Sector-Specific ETFs

Sector-specific ETFs invest in companies operating within a particular sector of the economy, such as technology, healthcare, or financial services. These ETFs provide exposure to all the major players within a sector, offering diversified risk within that specific segment. This allows investors to benefit from the collective growth of the entire sector while mitigating the risk associated with individual stocks.

Key Features of Sector-Specific ETFs:

1. **Focused Exposure:**
    - Sector ETFs provide concentrated exposure to industries expected to benefit from economic trends or specific growth drivers. For example, the **Technology Select Sector SPDR Fund (XLK)** focuses on the technology sector, including companies like Apple, Microsoft, and Alphabet.
2. **Diversification within the Sector:**
    - While sector ETFs are concentrated in one sector, they offer diversification within that sector by holding multiple stocks. This helps reduce the impact of poor performance

by any single company. For instance, the **Health Care Select Sector SPDR Fund (XLV)** includes a wide range of healthcare companies, from pharmaceuticals to medical devices.
3. **Economic and Market Cycles:**
    - Different sectors perform differently depending on economic cycles and market conditions. For example, defensive sectors like utilities and consumer staples tend to perform well during economic downturns, while cyclical sectors like technology and consumer discretionary may outperform during periods of economic growth.
4. **Strategic Allocation:**
    - Investors can use sector ETFs to overweight or underweight specific sectors in their portfolios based on their market outlook. This strategic allocation can enhance portfolio performance by capitalizing on sectors expected to outperform.

Examples of Sector-Specific ETFs:

- **Financial Select Sector SPDR Fund (XLF):**
    - This ETF focuses on the financial sector, including banks, investment firms, and insurance companies. XLF allows investors to capitalize on the performance of financial institutions, especially during periods of rising interest rates.
- **Energy Select Sector SPDR Fund (XLE):**
    - XLE provides exposure to the energy sector, including oil, gas, and energy equipment companies. This ETF can be a strategic investment during times of rising oil prices or increased demand for energy.
- **Industrial Select Sector SPDR Fund (XLI):**
    - Investing in the industrial sector, XLI includes companies involved in manufacturing, construction, and transportation. This ETF benefits from industrial growth driven by economic expansion and infrastructure development.

Conclusion

Sector-specific ETFs offer a powerful tool for investors looking to tailor their portfolios to specific sectors of the economy. By providing focused exposure, diversification within the sector, and the ability to strategically allocate investments based on economic and market cycles, these ETFs enable investors to take advantage of targeted growth opportunities while managing risk.

References:

1. "Sector ETFs: A Simple Way to Invest in the Economy's Top Performers" - Investopedia. Investopedia
2. "What Are Sector ETFs?" - The Balance. The Balance
3. "How to Invest in Sector ETFs" - Morningstar. Morningstar
4. "SPDR Sector ETFs" - State Street Global Advisors. SSGA

17.2 Performance and Risk Analysis

Sector and industry ETFs offer investors the opportunity to focus on specific segments of the market, potentially enhancing returns by capitalizing on sector-specific trends. However, this approach comes with its own set of performance considerations and risks that must be analyzed thoroughly.

Performance Analysis

1. Sector Rotation and Economic Cycles

- Sector ETFs often perform in line with their respective economic cycles. For instance, during periods of economic expansion, cyclical sectors like technology and consumer discretionary tend to outperform. Conversely, during economic downturns, defensive sectors such as utilities and consumer staples generally provide better performance. Understanding these cycles can help investors time their investments strategically.

- **Example:** The **Technology Select Sector SPDR Fund (XLK)** has historically outperformed during economic expansions due to high growth in tech companies. In contrast, the **Utilities Select Sector SPDR Fund (XLU)** tends to perform better during market downturns, offering stability and consistent dividends (Morningstar, SSGA).

2. Historical Performance Metrics

- Examining historical performance metrics, such as total return, standard deviation, and Sharpe ratio, can provide insights into the risk-adjusted returns of sector ETFs. Higher Sharpe ratios indicate better risk-adjusted performance.
- **Example:** Over the past five years, XLK has shown a higher annualized return compared to the broader S&P 500 index, reflecting the robust growth in the technology sector (Morningstar). However, its standard deviation is also higher, indicating greater volatility.

3. Benchmark Comparison

- Comparing sector ETFs to their respective benchmarks helps evaluate their performance. Many sector ETFs track well-known sector-specific indices, such as the S&P 500 sector indices. Performance relative to these benchmarks can indicate the effectiveness of the ETF's strategy.
- **Example:** The **Financial Select Sector SPDR Fund (XLF)** tracks the financial sector of the S&P 500. By comparing XLF's performance to the S&P 500 Financials Index, investors can assess how well the ETF captures the sector's performance (SSGA).

Risk Analysis

1. Concentration Risk

- Sector ETFs inherently carry concentration risk as they are heavily invested in one specific sector. This lack of diversification means

that any negative developments in the sector can significantly impact the ETF's performance.
- **Example:** The **Energy Select Sector SPDR Fund (XLE)** is highly exposed to fluctuations in oil prices. A sharp decline in oil prices can lead to substantial losses for XLE, as seen during the oil price crash in 2020 (Investopedia).

2. Volatility

- Sector ETFs can be more volatile than broad-market ETFs due to their focused exposure. Sectors like technology and biotechnology are particularly prone to high volatility due to rapid innovation and regulatory risks.
- **Example:** The **SPDR S&P Biotech ETF (XBI)** exhibits high volatility due to the inherent risks in biotech development and regulatory approvals. While it can offer high returns, it also carries the risk of significant price swings (SSGA).

3. Market Sentiment and External Factors

- Sector ETFs are susceptible to changes in market sentiment and external factors such as regulatory changes, geopolitical events, and technological advancements. These factors can create sudden and unpredictable impacts on sector performance.
- **Example:** The **Industrial Select Sector SPDR Fund (XLI)**, which invests in manufacturing and industrial companies, can be affected by trade policies and tariffs. Changes in international trade agreements or tariffs can influence the performance of industrial stocks (The Balance).

4. Liquidity Risk

- Liquidity risk can vary across sector ETFs. More popular sectors like technology and healthcare generally have higher liquidity, while niche sectors may face liquidity constraints, making it harder to buy or sell large quantities without affecting the price.
- **Example:** ETFs like **XLK** and **XLV** generally have high trading volumes, ensuring liquidity. However, more specialized ETFs may

experience lower trading volumes and wider bid-ask spreads, increasing transaction costs (Morningstar).

Conclusion

Sector and industry ETFs offer targeted exposure to specific areas of the market, allowing investors to capitalize on sector-specific growth trends. However, this focused approach also brings concentration risk, higher volatility, and sensitivity to market sentiment and external factors. By thoroughly analyzing performance metrics and understanding the associated risks, investors can make informed decisions and strategically incorporate sector ETFs into their portfolios.

17.3 Integration into Investment Portfolios

Integrating sector and industry ETFs into an investment portfolio can provide targeted exposure to specific areas of the market, helping investors to capitalize on sector-specific trends and diversify their holdings. Here's how to effectively integrate these ETFs into a broader investment strategy.

1. Strategic Allocation

Sector and industry ETFs can be used to strategically overweight or underweight specific sectors based on market outlook and economic cycles. For instance, an investor might overweight technology during periods of economic expansion due to higher growth potential, and underweight it during downturns to mitigate risk.

- **Example:** If an investor believes that the technology sector will outperform due to advancements in AI and cloud computing, they might allocate a larger portion of their portfolio to the **Technology Select Sector SPDR Fund (XLK)** (Morningstar, Investopedia).

2. Diversification

While sector ETFs concentrate investments within a particular sector, they still offer diversification within that sector by including multiple companies. This approach reduces the risk associated with investing in a single stock while allowing for sector-specific exposure.

- **Example:** The **Health Care Select Sector SPDR Fund (XLV)** includes a broad range of healthcare companies, from pharmaceuticals to medical device manufacturers, providing diversified exposure within the healthcare sector (SSGA).

3. Risk Management

Sector and industry ETFs can help manage risk by balancing high-growth sectors with more stable, defensive sectors. This strategy ensures that the portfolio is not overly exposed to market volatility or sector-specific downturns.

- **Example:** An investor might balance their portfolio by including both the **Consumer Staples Select Sector SPDR Fund (XLP)**, which is less volatile, and the **Consumer Discretionary Select Sector SPDR Fund (XLY)**, which has higher growth potential but also higher volatility (The Balance).

4. Tactical Adjustments

Investors can use sector ETFs for tactical adjustments based on short-term market opportunities or economic changes. This flexibility allows for quick reallocation without the need to buy or sell individual stocks.

- **Example:** During a market correction, an investor might increase their holdings in the **Utilities Select Sector SPDR Fund (XLU)** to take advantage of the sector's defensive nature, then shift back to more aggressive sectors once stability returns (Morningstar).

5. Thematic Investing

Sector ETFs can be integrated into thematic investing strategies, where the focus is on long-term trends rather than short-term market movements. This approach allows investors to target sectors expected to benefit from significant, lasting changes in the economy or society.

- **Example:** The **iShares Global Clean Energy ETF (ICLN)** can be included in a portfolio to capitalize on the global shift towards renewable energy and sustainability, reflecting a long-term commitment to green energy trends (BlackRock).

6. Core-Satellite Approach

In a core-satellite portfolio, broad-market index funds form the "core," providing stability and market exposure, while sector ETFs serve as "satellites," adding targeted exposure to specific sectors. This strategy combines the benefits of broad diversification with the potential for higher returns from selected sectors.

- **Example:** An investor might use the **Vanguard Total Stock Market ETF (VTI)** as the core holding and add sector ETFs like **XLK** for technology and **XLF** for financials as satellites to enhance returns (Investopedia).

Conclusion

Integrating sector and industry ETFs into an investment portfolio provides a versatile tool for targeting specific market segments, managing risk, and capitalizing on economic trends. By using strategic allocation, diversification, risk management, tactical adjustments, thematic investing, and the core-satellite approach, investors can effectively enhance their portfolios and achieve their financial goals.

18. ETFs in Retirement Accounts

Investing for retirement requires a strategic approach to ensure long-term growth and stability. Exchange-Traded Funds (ETFs) have become a popular choice for retirement accounts due to their cost-effectiveness, diversification benefits, and ease of management. Whether you're investing in an Individual Retirement Account (IRA), a 401(k), or other retirement savings plans, ETFs can play a crucial role in building a robust retirement portfolio. This chapter explores the advantages of including ETFs in retirement accounts and provides guidance on how to effectively integrate them into your retirement strategy.

18.1 Benefits of ETFs in Retirement Accounts

1. Cost-Effectiveness

One of the primary benefits of ETFs in retirement accounts is their low cost. ETFs typically have lower expense ratios compared to mutual funds, which means more of your investment returns are retained over time. This cost efficiency is particularly important in retirement accounts where long-term growth is crucial.

- **Example:** The **Vanguard Total Stock Market ETF (VTI)** has an expense ratio of just 0.03%, significantly lower than the average mutual fund, allowing more of your money to be invested and grow over time (Vanguard).

2. Diversification

ETFs offer instant diversification by pooling together a wide range of assets within a single fund. This diversification reduces the risk associated with individual stocks and sectors, providing a more stable investment vehicle for retirement savings.

- **Example:** The **iShares Core MSCI Total International Stock ETF (IXUS)** provides exposure to thousands of international stocks across various sectors and regions, enhancing the diversification of a retirement portfolio (BlackRock).

3. Tax Efficiency

ETFs are known for their tax efficiency, primarily due to their unique structure and the in-kind creation and redemption process. This process minimizes capital gains distributions, reducing the tax burden on investors and making ETFs particularly advantageous for taxable accounts. However, even in tax-advantaged retirement accounts, the tax efficiency of ETFs can help maximize after-tax returns.

- **Example:** The tax-efficient structure of ETFs, like those from **iShares** and **Vanguard**, allows investors to defer taxes until withdrawals are made, optimizing the growth potential within retirement accounts (Morningstar).

4. Flexibility and Accessibility

ETFs offer the flexibility of being traded like stocks on exchanges, allowing for intraday buying and selling. This accessibility makes it easier for investors to manage their portfolios and adjust their asset allocations as needed without waiting for the end-of-day pricing typical of mutual funds.

- **Example:** The ability to trade ETFs throughout the day can be particularly beneficial during periods of market volatility, enabling investors to react promptly to market changes (Investopedia).

5. Variety of Options

There is a vast array of ETFs available, covering a wide range of asset classes, sectors, and investment strategies. This variety allows investors to tailor their retirement portfolios to their specific risk tolerance and investment goals.

- **Example:** Investors can choose from broad market ETFs like the **SPDR S&P 500 ETF (SPY)**, sector-specific ETFs like the **Technology Select Sector SPDR Fund (XLK)**, or bond ETFs like the **iShares Core U.S. Aggregate Bond ETF (AGG)**, depending on their investment needs (SSGA, BlackRock).

6. Transparency

ETFs are highly transparent investment vehicles, with holdings disclosed on a daily basis. This transparency allows investors to see exactly what they own and make informed decisions about their portfolios.

- **Example:** Most ETFs, such as those from **Vanguard** and **iShares**, provide daily updates on their holdings, offering investors clear visibility into their investments (Vanguard, BlackRock).

Conclusion

ETFs offer numerous benefits for retirement accounts, including cost-effectiveness, diversification, tax efficiency, flexibility, variety, and transparency. These advantages make them a valuable component of a well-constructed retirement portfolio. By understanding and leveraging these benefits, investors can enhance their retirement savings strategy and work towards a secure and prosperous future.

References:

1. "Vanguard Total Stock Market ETF (VTI)" - Vanguard. Vanguard
2. "iShares Core MSCI Total International Stock ETF (IXUS)" - BlackRock. BlackRock
3. "Tax Efficiency of ETFs" - Morningstar. Morningstar
4. "Benefits of ETFs in Retirement Accounts" - Investopedia. Investopedia
5. "SPDR Sector ETFs" - State Street Global Advisors. SSGA

18.2 Strategies for Long-Term Growth

Building a robust retirement portfolio requires a thoughtful approach to ensure sustainable, long-term growth. ETFs provide a versatile and effective vehicle for achieving this goal. Here are several strategies for leveraging ETFs to enhance long-term growth in retirement accounts.

1. Diversified Core Holdings

A strong foundation for any retirement portfolio involves diversified core holdings. Broad-market ETFs that cover large segments of the market can serve as the cornerstone of your investment strategy, providing exposure to a wide range of assets.

- **Example:** The **Vanguard Total Stock Market ETF (VTI)** offers comprehensive exposure to the entire U.S. stock market, encompassing large-, mid-, and small-cap stocks across various sectors. This broad diversification helps reduce risk and provides steady growth potential over time (Vanguard).

2. Growth-Oriented Sector Allocation

Allocating a portion of the portfolio to growth-oriented sectors can enhance returns. Sectors such as technology, healthcare, and renewable energy have shown strong growth prospects and can provide significant upside potential.

- **Example:** The **Technology Select Sector SPDR Fund (XLK)** focuses on the technology sector, which has historically outperformed other sectors due to rapid innovation and high growth rates. Similarly, the **iShares Global Clean Energy ETF (ICLN)** targets the renewable energy sector, benefiting from the global shift towards sustainable energy sources (SSGA, BlackRock).

3. International Diversification

Including international ETFs in a retirement portfolio can provide exposure to growth opportunities outside the domestic market. International diversification helps mitigate country-specific risks and captures growth from emerging and developed markets globally.

- **Example:** The **iShares MSCI ACWI ex U.S. ETF (ACWX)** offers exposure to a broad range of international stocks, excluding the U.S., across both developed and emerging markets. This diversification enhances the growth potential of the portfolio by tapping into global economic growth (BlackRock).

4. Dividend Growth Strategy

Investing in ETFs that focus on companies with strong dividend growth records can provide a reliable income stream and capital appreciation. Dividend growth ETFs often include companies with solid financials and consistent dividend increases.

- **Example:** The **Vanguard Dividend Appreciation ETF (VIG)** targets companies that have a history of increasing dividends over time, providing a combination of income and growth. This approach can be particularly beneficial for retirees seeking steady income along with portfolio growth (Vanguard).

5. Bond ETFs for Stability

Incorporating bond ETFs into a retirement portfolio can provide stability and reduce overall portfolio volatility. Bond ETFs offer predictable income and act as a buffer against stock market fluctuations.

- **Example:** The **iShares Core U.S. Aggregate Bond ETF (AGG)** includes a diversified mix of U.S. investment-grade bonds, offering stability and income. This ETF can help balance the higher volatility of equity holdings and protect against downside risks (BlackRock).

6. Tactical Adjustments Based on Economic Conditions

Making tactical adjustments to the portfolio based on prevailing economic conditions can optimize returns. For instance, during periods of economic uncertainty, increasing exposure to defensive sectors or safe-haven assets can preserve capital.

- **Example:** During economic downturns, increasing holdings in the **Consumer Staples Select Sector SPDR Fund (XLP)**, which focuses on essential consumer goods, can provide stability. Conversely, during economic recoveries, shifting towards cyclical sectors like consumer discretionary can enhance growth potential (SSGA, Morningstar).

7. Rebalancing and Monitoring

Regularly rebalancing the portfolio ensures that the asset allocation remains aligned with the investor's risk tolerance and investment goals. Rebalancing helps maintain the desired exposure to various asset classes and sectors, preventing any one area from becoming too dominant.

- **Example:** Periodic rebalancing can involve adjusting the weights of ETFs like **VTI**, **XLK**, **AGG**, and others to maintain the target allocation. Monitoring the portfolio's performance and making necessary adjustments based on changes in market conditions and personal circumstances is crucial for long-term success (Investopedia).

Conclusion

Employing these strategies can help investors build a retirement portfolio that balances growth potential with stability and income. By incorporating diversified core holdings, growth-oriented sectors, international diversification, dividend growth, bond ETFs, tactical adjustments, and regular rebalancing, investors can create a robust portfolio designed for long-term growth and financial security in retirement.

18.3 Tax Advantages and Considerations

One of the significant benefits of incorporating ETFs into retirement accounts is their tax efficiency. Understanding the tax advantages and considerations is crucial for maximizing the growth and sustainability of your retirement savings.

ETFs, dangerous financial instruments?

1. Tax-Deferred Growth

Investing in ETFs within tax-advantaged retirement accounts, such as IRAs and 401(k)s, allows for tax-deferred growth. This means that you won't pay taxes on the earnings (dividends, interest, and capital gains) until you withdraw the funds during retirement. This deferral can significantly enhance the compounding effect, leading to substantial growth over the long term.

- **Example:** If you invest in a **Vanguard Total Stock Market ETF (VTI)** within an IRA, the dividends and capital gains generated by VTI will not be subject to taxes until you start making withdrawals. This tax deferral allows your investments to grow more efficiently over time (Vanguard).

2. Roth IRAs and Tax-Free Withdrawals

For Roth IRAs, the tax advantages are even more pronounced. Contributions to Roth IRAs are made with after-tax dollars, but qualified withdrawals during retirement are tax-free. This setup is highly beneficial for investors expecting to be in a higher tax bracket in retirement.

- **Example:** If you invest in an **iShares Core S&P 500 ETF (IVV)** within a Roth IRA, all dividends and capital gains grow tax-free. When you withdraw the funds in retirement, you won't owe any taxes on the distributions, allowing you to maximize your retirement income (BlackRock).

3. Capital Gains Tax Efficiency

ETFs are generally more tax-efficient than mutual funds due to their unique structure and the in-kind creation and redemption process. This process minimizes the realization of capital gains, thereby reducing the tax burden on investors. While this is primarily advantageous in taxable accounts, it also benefits retirement accounts by further minimizing any potential tax drag.

- **Example:** The **iShares Core U.S. Aggregate Bond ETF (AGG)** can be held in a retirement account without worrying about frequent capital gains distributions, as the ETF structure helps in managing and minimizing such distributions (BlackRock).

4. Required Minimum Distributions (RMDs)

One consideration for traditional IRAs and 401(k) accounts is the requirement to take minimum distributions starting at age 73 (as of 2023). While ETFs themselves do not have specific RMD rules, the funds held within these accounts are subject to RMDs. Failing to take RMDs can result in significant penalties.

- **Example:** If you have a substantial portion of your retirement savings in **SPDR S&P 500 ETF (SPY)** within a traditional IRA, you need to ensure that you take the required distributions each year starting at age 73 to avoid penalties (SSGA).

5. Conversion Strategies

Investors might consider converting traditional IRAs to Roth IRAs to benefit from tax-free withdrawals in retirement. This strategy involves paying taxes on the converted amount now, but allows the investments to grow tax-free thereafter. ETFs can be an excellent vehicle for this strategy due to their tax efficiency and growth potential.

- **Example:** Converting a portion of your traditional IRA holdings, such as the **Invesco QQQ ETF (QQQ)**, to a Roth IRA could be beneficial if you expect higher tax rates in the future. The growth of QQQ within the Roth IRA would be tax-free, and future withdrawals would not be subject to taxes (Invesco).

6. Estate Planning Considerations

ETFs held in retirement accounts also offer benefits for estate planning. For instance, Roth IRAs are not subject to RMDs during the account holder's lifetime, making them an effective tool for wealth transfer.

Additionally, ETFs generally have low turnover, reducing the tax impact on beneficiaries.

- **Example:** Holding a diversified ETF like the **iShares MSCI ACWI ETF (ACWI)** in a Roth IRA can be a strategic part of an estate plan, ensuring that the beneficiaries receive the assets without immediate tax consequences (BlackRock).

Conclusion

ETFs offer numerous tax advantages when incorporated into retirement accounts, including tax-deferred growth, tax-free withdrawals in Roth accounts, and overall tax efficiency. By understanding these benefits and considerations, investors can optimize their retirement strategies and enhance their financial security in retirement.

19. Leveraged and Inverse ETFs

Leveraged and inverse ETFs are specialized financial instruments designed to amplify returns or provide inverse performance relative to a specific benchmark or index. These ETFs are popular among sophisticated investors and traders who seek to capitalize on short-term market movements or hedge existing positions. However, they come with heightened risks and complexities that require a thorough understanding before inclusion in an investment strategy. This chapter delves into the mechanics of leveraged and inverse ETFs, explaining how they work and the unique risks and opportunities they present.

19.1 How They Work

Leveraged ETFs

Leveraged ETFs aim to deliver multiples of the performance of the underlying index for a single day. For example, a 2x leveraged ETF seeks to produce twice the daily return of the index it tracks. These ETFs achieve their objectives through the use of financial derivatives such as futures contracts, options, and swaps.

- **Example:** The **ProShares Ultra S&P 500 ETF (SSO)** is a 2x leveraged ETF that aims to return twice the daily performance of the S&P 500 Index. If the S&P 500 increases by 1% in a day, SSO is designed to increase by 2% on that same day (ProShares).

Leveraged ETFs reset their leverage on a daily basis, meaning that the intended leverage factor is maintained only for one trading day. Over longer periods, the returns can deviate significantly from the multiple of the index due to the effects of compounding. This makes leveraged ETFs suitable primarily for short-term trading rather than long-term holding.

Inverse ETFs

Inverse ETFs are designed to provide the opposite performance of the underlying index for a single day. They achieve this by using derivatives to create short exposure to the index. Inverse ETFs are often used by investors to hedge against declines in the market or to speculate on downward market movements.

- **Example:** The **ProShares Short S&P 500 ETF (SH)** is an inverse ETF that seeks to return the opposite of the daily performance of the S&P 500 Index. If the S&P 500 falls by 1% in a day, SH is designed to increase by 1% on that same day (ProShares).

Like leveraged ETFs, inverse ETFs reset daily, and their performance over longer periods can deviate from the inverse of the index due to the effects of compounding. Therefore, they are best used for short-term strategies.

Mechanics and Strategies

Leveraged and inverse ETFs use complex financial instruments to achieve their objectives. These instruments include:

1. **Futures Contracts:** Agreements to buy or sell a particular asset at a predetermined price at a specified time in the future. They are commonly used to gain exposure to indexes and commodities.

2. **Options:** Contracts that give the holder the right, but not the obligation, to buy or sell an asset at a specified price before a certain date. Options can be used to leverage exposure and hedge risks.
3. **Swaps:** Contracts in which two parties agree to exchange cash flows or other financial instruments. Total return swaps are frequently used to provide leverage and inverse exposure.

These instruments allow leveraged and inverse ETFs to magnify returns or provide inverse performance but also introduce additional risks, such as counterparty risk, liquidity risk, and tracking error.

Conclusion

Understanding how leveraged and inverse ETFs work is crucial for any investor considering their use. These ETFs can be powerful tools for short-term trading strategies and hedging, but they come with significant risks and complexities. Investors must be aware of the daily reset feature, the impact of compounding on returns, and the inherent risks associated with the derivatives used in these funds. With proper knowledge and strategy, leveraged and inverse ETFs can be effectively integrated into an investment portfolio for tactical purposes.

References:

1. "What Are Leveraged and Inverse ETFs?" - Investopedia. Investopedia
2. "ProShares Ultra S&P 500 ETF (SSO)" - ProShares. ProShares
3. "ProShares Short S&P 500 ETF (SH)" - ProShares. ProShares
4. "Understanding Leveraged and Inverse ETFs" - SEC. SEC
5. "Leveraged and Inverse ETFs: Not for the Faint of Heart" - FINRA. FINRA

19.2 Risks and Rewards

Leveraged and inverse ETFs offer unique opportunities for investors to amplify returns or hedge against market downturns, but they also come with significant risks. Understanding the balance between these risks and rewards is crucial for any investor considering these complex instruments.

Rewards

1. **Amplified Returns**
    - Leveraged ETFs aim to provide multiples of the daily performance of the underlying index. For example, a 2x leveraged ETF seeks to return twice the daily performance. This can result in substantial gains during bullish market periods.
    - **Example:** The **ProShares UltraPro QQQ ETF (TQQQ)** seeks to deliver three times the daily performance of the Nasdaq-100 Index. During periods of strong market performance, TQQQ can provide significantly higher returns compared to non-leveraged ETFs (ProShares).
2. **Short-Term Hedging**
    - Inverse ETFs allow investors to profit from declines in the underlying index. They can be used as a hedging tool to protect against market downturns or to capitalize on bearish market conditions.
    - **Example:** The **ProShares Short S&P 500 ETF (SH)** seeks to provide the inverse of the daily performance of the S&P 500 Index. Investors anticipating a market decline can use SH to offset losses in their long positions (ProShares).
3. **Strategic Flexibility**
    - Leveraged and inverse ETFs offer flexibility for sophisticated trading strategies. They can be used to quickly adjust exposure based on market outlook, allowing for tactical moves without the need for margin accounts or complex derivatives.
    - **Example:** Traders can use leveraged ETFs to amplify exposure to sectors expected to outperform in the short term, such as using the **Direxion Daily Financial Bull 3X Shares (FAS)** for a bullish view on the financial sector (Direxion).

ETFs, dangerous financial instruments?

Risks

1. **Compounding Effects**
   - The daily reset feature of leveraged and inverse ETFs can lead to significant deviations from the expected multiple or inverse performance over longer periods. Compounding can cause these ETFs to underperform their targets, especially in volatile markets.
   - **Example:** Over time, the performance of a 2x leveraged ETF may not be exactly double the return of the underlying index due to the effects of daily compounding. This can be detrimental in volatile markets where frequent price fluctuations erode returns (SEC).
2. **Increased Volatility**
   - Leveraged and inverse ETFs are inherently more volatile than their non-leveraged counterparts. The use of derivatives such as futures and swaps introduces additional layers of risk, including market, liquidity, and counterparty risks.
   - **Example:** The **ProShares Ultra VIX Short-Term Futures ETF (UVXY)**, which seeks to provide twice the daily performance of the S&P 500 VIX Short-Term Futures Index, can experience extreme volatility, making it suitable only for short-term strategies (ProShares).
3. **Decay and Erosion**
   - Leveraged and inverse ETFs can suffer from decay due to daily rebalancing and the costs associated with maintaining leveraged positions. This decay can erode returns over time, particularly in choppy markets where the index fluctuates frequently.
   - **Example:** In a volatile sideways market, the performance of the **Direxion Daily S&P 500 Bear 3X Shares (SPXS)** may not meet investor expectations due to the continuous rebalancing required to maintain its leverage (Direxion).
4. **Complexity and Misunderstanding**
   - These ETFs are complex financial instruments that may not be suitable for all investors. Misunderstanding their mechanics can lead to significant losses. They are typically

recommended for experienced traders who can actively monitor and manage their positions.
- **Example:** Many investors fail to grasp the short-term nature of these products, leading to unexpected losses. The **FINRA** and **SEC** have issued warnings about the risks of leveraged and inverse ETFs, emphasizing the importance of understanding these products before investing (FINRA, SEC).

Conclusion

Leveraged and inverse ETFs offer potent tools for amplifying returns and hedging against market downturns, but they come with heightened risks, including compounding effects, increased volatility, and potential for decay. These products are best suited for sophisticated investors who have a deep understanding of their mechanics and are prepared for active management. Properly utilized, they can enhance a portfolio's tactical flexibility and potential returns, but they require careful consideration and risk management.

19.3 Suitability for Different Types of Investors

Leveraged and inverse ETFs are specialized financial instruments designed for short-term trading and sophisticated investment strategies. These products are not suitable for all investors due to their complexity, higher risk, and the potential for significant losses. Understanding which types of investors can benefit from these ETFs, and which should avoid them, is crucial for effective portfolio management.

1. Sophisticated Traders and Active Investors

Ideal For:

- Leveraged and inverse ETFs are best suited for sophisticated traders and active investors who have a deep understanding of financial markets and the specific mechanics of these products.

ETFs, dangerous financial instruments?

These investors are typically experienced in using derivatives and have a high tolerance for risk.
- **Example:** Day traders and short-term traders who seek to capitalize on daily market movements and have the ability to monitor their investments closely throughout the trading day. They can use products like the **ProShares UltraPro QQQ ETF (TQQQ)** for bullish strategies or the **ProShares UltraPro Short QQQ ETF (SQQQ)** for bearish strategies on the Nasdaq-100 Index (ProShares).

2. Institutional Investors and Hedge Funds

Ideal For:

- Institutional investors and hedge funds often employ sophisticated strategies that can benefit from the leverage and inverse exposure provided by these ETFs. They have the resources and expertise to manage the risks associated with these instruments.
- **Example:** Hedge funds might use leveraged ETFs like the **Direxion Daily Financial Bull 3X Shares (FAS)** to amplify their exposure to the financial sector during bullish periods, or inverse ETFs like the **Direxion Daily Financial Bear 3X Shares (FAZ)** to hedge against market downturns (Direxion).

3. Market Timing and Tactical Allocation Investors

Ideal For:

- Investors who engage in market timing and tactical allocation can use leveraged and inverse ETFs to adjust their portfolio exposures based on short-term market outlooks. These investors use these ETFs to gain targeted exposure without the need to trade individual stocks or use margin accounts.
- **Example:** A tactical allocator might increase exposure to the energy sector using the **ProShares Ultra Oil & Gas ETF (DIG)** during periods of rising oil prices, or hedge against a downturn with the **ProShares UltraShort Oil & Gas ETF (DUG)** (ProShares).

4. Not Suitable For:

Long-Term, Buy-and-Hold Investors:

- Leveraged and inverse ETFs are generally not suitable for long-term, buy-and-hold investors due to the effects of daily compounding and potential for significant deviation from the underlying index over extended periods.
- **Example:** Investors who seek stable, long-term growth and are focused on retirement savings or conservative investment strategies should avoid these products. For such investors, traditional broad-market ETFs like the **Vanguard Total Stock Market ETF (VTI)** or the **iShares Core S&P 500 ETF (IVV)** are more appropriate (Vanguard, BlackRock).

Retirement Account Investors:

- Due to their inherent risks and volatility, leveraged and inverse ETFs are typically unsuitable for retirement accounts where preservation of capital and steady growth are primary objectives.
- **Example:** Investors saving for retirement are better served with diversified, low-cost ETFs that provide broad market exposure and minimize risk, such as the **iShares MSCI ACWI ETF (ACWI)** (BlackRock).

Novice Investors:

- New and inexperienced investors should avoid leveraged and inverse ETFs because they require a sophisticated understanding of market mechanics and the ability to manage high levels of risk.
- **Example:** Novice investors are better off starting with simpler investment vehicles, like target-date funds or diversified index ETFs, to build a solid foundation before considering more complex instruments (Investopedia).

Conclusion

Leveraged and inverse ETFs can be powerful tools for certain types of investors, particularly sophisticated traders, institutional investors, and those engaged in tactical allocation strategies. However, they are generally unsuitable for long-term, buy-and-hold investors, retirement accounts, and novice investors due to their complexity and risk. Proper education, experience, and risk management are essential for those considering these specialized ETFs.

Part VI: Practical Applications

20. Building a Portfolio with ETFs

Building a well-structured investment portfolio is crucial for achieving long-term financial goals while managing risk effectively. Exchange-Traded Funds (ETFs) offer an excellent vehicle for constructing diversified, cost-efficient, and flexible portfolios. Whether you are a novice investor or an experienced trader, understanding the principles of portfolio construction and how to leverage ETFs can significantly enhance your investment strategy. This section provides a comprehensive guide to building a portfolio with ETFs, from initial planning to ongoing management.

20.1 Step-by-Step Guide to Portfolio Construction

Step 1: Define Your Investment Goals

The first step in building a portfolio is to clearly define your investment goals. Consider what you are investing for—retirement, a major purchase, education, or wealth accumulation. Your goals will influence your investment horizon, risk tolerance, and the types of ETFs suitable for your portfolio.

- **Example:** If you are investing for retirement with a long-term horizon, you might prioritize growth-oriented ETFs and have a higher risk tolerance. Conversely, if you are saving for a short-term goal, you might opt for more conservative, income-generating ETFs.

Step 2: Assess Your Risk Tolerance

Understanding your risk tolerance is critical in determining the appropriate asset allocation for your portfolio. Risk tolerance is influenced by factors such as your investment horizon, financial situation, and personal comfort with market volatility.

- **Example:** Use tools like risk assessment questionnaires or consult with a financial advisor to gauge your risk tolerance. Websites like Vanguard and Fidelity offer risk tolerance tools that can help you assess your comfort level with different types of investment risks.

Step 3: Determine Asset Allocation

Asset allocation involves spreading your investments across various asset classes (stocks, bonds, real estate, etc.) to balance risk and reward according to your risk tolerance and investment goals. ETFs make it easy to diversify within and across asset classes.

- **Example:** A typical balanced portfolio might include 60% equities and 40% bonds. Within equities, you might allocate 40% to U.S. stocks and 20% to international stocks. For bonds, you might choose a mix of government and corporate bonds.

Step 4: Select Appropriate ETFs

Once you have determined your asset allocation, select ETFs that match your allocation strategy. Consider factors such as expense ratios, liquidity, tracking error, and the underlying index.

- **Example:** For U.S. equities, you might choose the **Vanguard Total Stock Market ETF (VTI)** for broad market exposure. For international stocks, the **iShares MSCI ACWI ex U.S. ETF (ACWX)** provides comprehensive global coverage. For bonds, the **iShares Core U.S. Aggregate Bond ETF (AGG)** offers diversified fixed-income exposure.

Step 5: Implement the Portfolio

After selecting the appropriate ETFs, implement your portfolio by purchasing the ETFs through your brokerage account. Ensure you have a well-balanced mix according to your asset allocation plan.

- **Example:** If your asset allocation calls for 60% in equities and 40% in bonds, and your total investment amount is $10,000, you would invest $6,000 in equity ETFs and $4,000 in bond ETFs.

Step 6: Monitor and Rebalance Regularly

Regular monitoring and rebalancing are essential to maintain your desired asset allocation. Market movements can cause your portfolio to drift from its target allocation, increasing risk or reducing potential returns.

- **Example:** Review your portfolio quarterly or annually. If equities have grown and now represent 70% of your portfolio instead of the intended 60%, sell a portion of the equity ETFs and reinvest in bond ETFs to restore the balance.

Step 7: Adjust for Changing Goals and Market Conditions

Over time, your investment goals and market conditions may change. Adjust your portfolio accordingly to stay aligned with your objectives and risk tolerance.

- **Example:** As you approach retirement, you might shift from growth-oriented ETFs to more conservative, income-focused ETFs. Alternatively, if market conditions indicate a potential downturn, you might increase your allocation to defensive sectors or bond ETFs.

Conclusion

Building a portfolio with ETFs involves careful planning, disciplined implementation, and ongoing management. By following these steps—defining goals, assessing risk tolerance, determining asset

ETFs, dangerous financial instruments?

allocation, selecting ETFs, implementing the portfolio, monitoring and rebalancing, and adjusting for changes—you can create a diversified and resilient portfolio tailored to your financial objectives.

References:

1. "How to Build a Portfolio with ETFs" - Investopedia. Investopedia
2. "ETFs: The Basics" - Vanguard. Vanguard
3. "Asset Allocation and Diversification" - Fidelity. Fidelity

20.2 Sample Portfolios for Different Risk Profiles

Creating a diversified portfolio tailored to your risk tolerance is crucial for achieving your financial goals while managing risk effectively. Below are sample portfolios designed for three different risk profiles: conservative, moderate, and aggressive. Each portfolio includes a mix of ETFs that provide broad diversification and align with the investor's risk tolerance.

1. Conservative Portfolio

A conservative portfolio is designed for investors with a low risk tolerance, such as those nearing retirement or who prioritize capital preservation. This portfolio emphasizes stability and income, with a higher allocation to bonds and lower exposure to equities.

Asset Allocation:

- **40% Equities**
    - **20% U.S. Stocks:** Vanguard Dividend Appreciation ETF (VIG)
    - **10% International Stocks:** iShares MSCI EAFE ETF (EFA)
    - **10% Real Estate:** Vanguard Real Estate ETF (VNQ)
- **60% Bonds**
    - **40% U.S. Bonds:** iShares Core U.S. Aggregate Bond ETF (AGG)
    - **10% International Bonds:** Vanguard Total International Bond ETF (BNDX)

- **10% Short-Term Bonds:** iShares Short Treasury Bond ETF (SHV)

Example Allocation:

- **Vanguard Dividend Appreciation ETF (VIG):** Focuses on U.S. companies with a history of increasing dividends, providing stable returns and income (Vanguard).
- **iShares MSCI EAFE ETF (EFA):** Offers exposure to large- and mid-cap companies in developed markets outside the U.S. and Canada, adding international diversification (BlackRock).
- **iShares Core U.S. Aggregate Bond ETF (AGG):** A broad-based bond ETF that provides exposure to U.S. investment-grade bonds, offering stability and income (BlackRock).

2. Moderate Portfolio

A moderate portfolio is suitable for investors with a balanced risk tolerance who seek a mix of growth and income. This portfolio balances equities and bonds, aiming for steady growth with moderate risk.

Asset Allocation:

- **60% Equities**
    - **30% U.S. Stocks:** Vanguard Total Stock Market ETF (VTI)
    - **15% International Stocks:** iShares MSCI ACWI ex U.S. ETF (ACWX)
    - **15% Sector-Specific ETFs:** Technology Select Sector SPDR Fund (XLK)
- **40% Bonds**
    - **30% U.S. Bonds:** iShares Core U.S. Aggregate Bond ETF (AGG)
    - **10% High-Yield Bonds:** SPDR Bloomberg Barclays High Yield Bond ETF (JNK)

Example Allocation:

- **Vanguard Total Stock Market ETF (VTI):** Provides broad exposure to the entire U.S. stock market, including large-, mid-, and small-cap stocks (Vanguard).
- **iShares MSCI ACWI ex U.S. ETF (ACWX):** Offers global diversification by investing in companies outside the U.S., including emerging markets (BlackRock).
- **Technology Select Sector SPDR Fund (XLK):** Focuses on the technology sector, which has high growth potential (SSGA).

3. Aggressive Portfolio

An aggressive portfolio is designed for investors with a high risk tolerance who seek maximum growth. This portfolio has a higher allocation to equities and minimal exposure to bonds, suitable for long-term investors who can withstand market volatility.

Asset Allocation:

- **80% Equities**
    - **50% U.S. Stocks:** iShares Core S&P 500 ETF (IVV)
    - **20% International Stocks:** Vanguard FTSE Emerging Markets ETF (VWO)
    - **10% Thematic ETFs:** ARK Innovation ETF (ARKK)
- **20% Bonds**
    - **10% U.S. Bonds:** Vanguard Total Bond Market ETF (BND)
    - **10% International Bonds:** iShares J.P. Morgan USD Emerging Markets Bond ETF (EMB)

Example Allocation:

- **iShares Core S&P 500 ETF (IVV):** Provides exposure to 500 of the largest U.S. companies, offering a strong foundation for growth (BlackRock).
- **Vanguard FTSE Emerging Markets ETF (VWO):** Targets stocks in emerging markets, providing higher growth potential and diversification (Vanguard).

- **ARK Innovation ETF (ARKK):** Invests in disruptive innovation across various sectors, such as technology and healthcare, aiming for high returns (ARK Invest).

Conclusion

These sample portfolios offer a starting point for constructing diversified portfolios tailored to different risk profiles. By selecting appropriate ETFs and adjusting the asset allocation according to your risk tolerance and investment goals, you can create a portfolio that balances risk and reward effectively. Regular monitoring and rebalancing are essential to maintain alignment with your financial objectives.

20.3 Rebalancing and Monitoring Your Portfolio

Building a portfolio is just the first step in your investment journey. To ensure your portfolio continues to align with your financial goals and risk tolerance, regular monitoring and rebalancing are crucial. This process helps manage risk, maintain your desired asset allocation, and optimize performance over the long term.

1. Importance of Monitoring Your Portfolio

Regularly monitoring your portfolio involves reviewing your investments to ensure they continue to meet your objectives. This includes tracking performance, evaluating market conditions, and assessing any changes in your personal financial situation.

- **Performance Tracking:** Regularly review the performance of your ETFs relative to their benchmarks. This helps you understand how well your investments are performing and if any adjustments are necessary.
    - **Example:** Use tools provided by your brokerage or financial platforms like Morningstar to track the performance of ETFs such as the **Vanguard Total Stock Market ETF (VTI)** or the **iShares MSCI ACWI ex U.S. ETF (ACWX)** (Morningstar).

- **Market Conditions:** Stay informed about market trends and economic indicators that may impact your investments. Changes in interest rates, inflation, or geopolitical events can influence the performance of different asset classes.
    - **Example:** Subscribe to financial news services or use platforms like Bloomberg and CNBC to stay updated on market conditions and economic forecasts (Bloomberg, CNBC).
- **Personal Financial Situation:** Reevaluate your financial goals, risk tolerance, and investment horizon regularly. Major life events such as retirement, job changes, or significant expenses may necessitate adjustments to your portfolio.

2. Rebalancing Your Portfolio

Rebalancing involves adjusting your portfolio back to its target asset allocation to manage risk and ensure it aligns with your investment strategy. Over time, market movements can cause your portfolio to drift from its original allocation, increasing risk or altering your intended investment profile.

- **Step-by-Step Rebalancing Process:**
    - **Determine the Frequency:** Decide how often to rebalance your portfolio. Common intervals include quarterly, semi-annually, or annually. Alternatively, you can rebalance based on a specific threshold, such as a 5% deviation from your target allocation.
        - **Example:** If your target allocation is 60% equities and 40% bonds, and your equity allocation grows to 65%, it's time to rebalance.
    - **Review Current Allocation:** Assess your current asset allocation to identify any significant deviations from your target. Use your brokerage account or financial software to view your portfolio's current composition.
        - **Example:** If the **Vanguard Total Stock Market ETF (VTI)** has significantly outperformed, it may now represent a larger portion of your portfolio than intended.

- **Buy and Sell Assets:** Adjust your holdings by selling overweight assets and buying underweight ones to restore your desired allocation.
    - **Example:** Sell a portion of **VTI** and use the proceeds to buy more of the **iShares Core U.S. Aggregate Bond ETF (AGG)** if bonds have become underrepresented.
- **Consider Tax Implications:** Be mindful of potential tax consequences when selling assets in taxable accounts. Use tax-advantaged accounts for rebalancing when possible to minimize tax impact.
    - **Example:** Rebalance within an IRA or 401(k) to avoid triggering capital gains taxes.

3. Tools and Resources for Monitoring and Rebalancing

Several tools and resources can help streamline the process of monitoring and rebalancing your portfolio:

- **Brokerage Platforms:** Most brokerage platforms offer portfolio tracking and rebalancing tools that provide insights into your current allocation and performance. Examples include Vanguard, Fidelity, and Schwab.
- **Financial Software:** Tools like Personal Capital, Morningstar Portfolio Manager, and Quicken offer comprehensive portfolio management features, including performance tracking and rebalancing recommendations (Personal Capital, Morningstar).
- **Robo-Advisors:** Robo-advisors like Betterment and Wealthfront automatically rebalance your portfolio based on your risk tolerance and goals, making the process hands-free (Betterment, Wealthfront).

Conclusion

Regular monitoring and rebalancing are essential practices for maintaining a healthy investment portfolio. By keeping track of your portfolio's performance, staying informed about market conditions, and adjusting your asset allocation as needed, you can manage risk and optimize returns.

Utilizing available tools and resources can simplify these tasks, ensuring that your portfolio remains aligned with your financial goals and risk tolerance.

21. ETFs in Different Market Conditions

Navigating the financial markets requires a dynamic approach, especially when using Exchange-Traded Funds (ETFs). Different market conditions, such as bull and bear markets, necessitate varying strategies to optimize returns and manage risk. This section explores how investors can leverage ETFs to adjust their portfolios based on prevailing market conditions, providing strategies for both bullish and bearish scenarios. Understanding these strategies helps investors make informed decisions, enhancing their ability to achieve long-term financial goals despite market fluctuations.

21.1 Strategies for Bull and Bear Markets

Bull Markets

A bull market is characterized by rising asset prices, typically driven by strong economic indicators, high investor confidence, and favorable market conditions. During bull markets, investors aim to maximize returns by capitalizing on the upward momentum. Here are some strategies to consider:

1. **Growth-Oriented ETFs**
     - Growth ETFs focus on companies expected to grow at an above-average rate compared to other companies. These ETFs are ideal during bull markets when risk appetite is higher.
     - **Example:** The **Vanguard Growth ETF (VUG)** targets large-cap growth stocks, offering exposure to high-growth companies in sectors like technology and consumer discretionary (Vanguard).

2. **Sector-Specific ETFs**
   - Certain sectors tend to outperform in bull markets, such as technology, consumer discretionary, and financials. Sector-specific ETFs can help investors capitalize on these trends.
   - **Example:** The **Technology Select Sector SPDR Fund (XLK)** provides targeted exposure to tech companies, which often lead market rallies during bullish phases (SSGA).
3. **Leveraged ETFs**
   - For experienced investors, leveraged ETFs can amplify returns by providing multiples of the daily performance of the underlying index.
   - **Example:** The **ProShares Ultra S&P 500 ETF (SSO)** seeks to deliver twice the daily performance of the S&P 500 Index, suitable for those looking to maximize gains in a rising market (ProShares).

Bear Markets

A bear market is defined by declining asset prices, often triggered by economic downturns, high levels of uncertainty, and low investor confidence. In bear markets, the focus shifts to preserving capital and mitigating losses. Here are some strategies for bear markets:

1. **Defensive Sector ETFs**
   - Defensive sectors, such as utilities, consumer staples, and healthcare, tend to be less volatile and more stable during market downturns. Investing in ETFs that focus on these sectors can help protect the portfolio.
   - **Example:** The **Utilities Select Sector SPDR Fund (XLU)** offers exposure to utility companies, which provide essential services and tend to perform better during economic slowdowns (SSGA).
2. **Inverse ETFs**
   - Inverse ETFs aim to provide the opposite performance of the underlying index, allowing investors to profit from market declines or hedge against potential losses.

- **Example:** The **ProShares Short S&P 500 ETF (SH)** seeks to deliver the inverse of the daily performance of the S&P 500 Index, making it a useful tool for hedging in a bear market (ProShares).

3. **Bond ETFs**
   - Bonds generally perform better than stocks in bear markets due to their lower risk and fixed income. Allocating a portion of the portfolio to bond ETFs can provide stability and income.
   - **Example:** The **iShares Core U.S. Aggregate Bond ETF (AGG)** offers broad exposure to U.S. investment-grade bonds, providing a safe haven during market volatility (BlackRock).

4. **Gold and Precious Metals ETFs**
   - Precious metals like gold are considered safe-haven assets, often increasing in value during market downturns. Gold ETFs provide an easy way to gain exposure to this asset class.
   - **Example:** The **SPDR Gold Shares ETF (GLD)** tracks the price of gold, offering a hedge against market and economic instability (SPDR).

Conclusion

Adapting your investment strategy to different market conditions using ETFs can enhance your portfolio's performance and resilience. By employing growth-oriented and sector-specific ETFs in bull markets and shifting to defensive, inverse, bond, and gold ETFs in bear markets, investors can better navigate the complexities of the financial markets. Regular monitoring and adjusting of your portfolio according to market conditions will help ensure long-term success and stability.

References:

1. "How to Invest in Bull and Bear Markets with ETFs" - Investopedia. Investopedia
2. "Vanguard Growth ETF (VUG)" - Vanguard. Vanguard

3. "Technology Select Sector SPDR Fund (XLK)" - State Street Global Advisors. SSGA
4. "ProShares Ultra S&P 500 ETF (SSO)" - ProShares. ProShares
5. "Utilities Select Sector SPDR Fund (XLU)" - State Street Global Advisors. SSGA
6. "ProShares Short S&P 500 ETF (SH)" - ProShares. ProShares
7. "iShares Core U.S. Aggregate Bond ETF (AGG)" - BlackRock. BlackRock
8. "SPDR Gold Shares ETF (GLD)" - SPDR. SPDR

21.2 Using ETFs for Hedging and Risk Management

Hedging and risk management are critical components of a robust investment strategy, particularly during periods of market uncertainty and volatility. ETFs offer a versatile and efficient way to hedge against potential losses and manage risk within a portfolio. This section explores various strategies for using ETFs to protect your investments and stabilize returns.

1. Inverse ETFs for Downside Protection

Inverse ETFs are designed to provide the opposite performance of a specific index or benchmark. They are particularly useful for hedging against market downturns, allowing investors to profit from declines in the underlying index.

- **Example:** The **ProShares Short S&P 500 ETF (SH)** seeks to deliver the inverse of the daily performance of the S&P 500 Index. By holding SH, investors can hedge against potential losses in their long positions in S&P 500 stocks (ProShares).

Advantages:

- Provides a straightforward way to gain short exposure without the need for margin accounts or short selling.
- Offers liquidity and ease of trading similar to traditional ETFs.

ETFs, dangerous financial instruments?

Considerations:

- Designed for short-term hedging due to daily reset feature, which can lead to tracking error over longer periods.
- Investors must actively manage positions to avoid unintended long-term performance deviations.

2. Sector-Specific ETFs for Targeted Hedging

Investors can use sector-specific ETFs to hedge exposure to particular sectors that may be vulnerable to market risks or economic downturns. By shorting sector ETFs or using inverse sector ETFs, investors can protect against declines in those sectors.

- **Example:** The **ProShares UltraShort Financials ETF (SKF)** provides twice the inverse daily performance of the Dow Jones U.S. Financials Index. This ETF can be used to hedge against declines in the financial sector during periods of economic uncertainty or rising interest rates (ProShares).

Advantages:

- Allows for targeted risk management by focusing on specific sectors.
- Flexibility to adjust exposure based on sector-specific outlooks and risks.

Considerations:

- Sector ETFs may exhibit higher volatility, requiring careful monitoring and management.
- Similar to inverse ETFs, these products are best suited for short-term strategies due to daily reset features.

3. Bond ETFs for Portfolio Stability

Incorporating bond ETFs into an equity-heavy portfolio can provide stability and income, particularly during periods of market volatility. Bond

ETFs typically exhibit lower volatility compared to equities, helping to reduce overall portfolio risk.

- **Example:** The **iShares Core U.S. Aggregate Bond ETF (AGG)** offers broad exposure to U.S. investment-grade bonds, providing a stable income stream and acting as a hedge against equity market declines (BlackRock).

Advantages:

- Diversifies risk by adding fixed-income exposure to the portfolio.
- Helps to balance the risk-return profile, especially during market downturns.

Considerations:

- Bond ETFs are subject to interest rate risk, which can impact their performance.
- Investors should consider the duration and credit quality of bond ETFs to align with their risk tolerance.

4. Commodity ETFs for Inflation Hedging

Commodity ETFs, particularly those focused on precious metals like gold, can serve as a hedge against inflation and economic uncertainty. These assets often retain or increase in value during periods of inflation or market stress.

- **Example:** The **SPDR Gold Shares ETF (GLD)** tracks the price of gold and provides a hedge against inflation and currency risk. Investors can use GLD to protect their portfolios from the erosive effects of inflation (SPDR).

Advantages:

- Provides a hedge against inflation and currency fluctuations.
- Offers diversification benefits due to low correlation with traditional asset classes.

Considerations:

- Commodity ETFs can be volatile and may not generate income.
- Investors need to be aware of storage costs and potential regulatory changes affecting commodities.

5. Volatility ETFs for Market Turbulence

Volatility ETFs, such as those tracking the VIX (Volatility Index), can be used to hedge against market volatility. These ETFs typically rise in value when market volatility increases, offering protection during turbulent market conditions.

- **Example:** The **ProShares VIX Short-Term Futures ETF (VIXY)** aims to provide exposure to the S&P 500 VIX Short-Term Futures Index, which measures market volatility expectations. VIXY can be used to hedge against spikes in market volatility (ProShares).

Advantages:

- Provides a direct hedge against market volatility.
- Useful for protecting portfolios during periods of market stress and uncertainty.

Considerations:

- Volatility ETFs are complex and can be highly volatile themselves.
- These ETFs are designed for short-term use and require active management to avoid decay and tracking error.

Conclusion

ETFs offer a range of tools for hedging and risk management, from inverse and sector-specific ETFs to bond, commodity, and volatility ETFs. By incorporating these instruments into their portfolios, investors can protect against market downturns, stabilize returns, and manage risks more effectively. However, it's essential to understand the specific characteristics and risks of each type of ETF and to use them appropriately within the context of a broader investment strategy.

21.3 Case Studies of ETFs in Market Crises

Exchange-Traded Funds (ETFs) have been tested through various market crises, demonstrating both their resilience and vulnerabilities. This section examines specific case studies of how different ETFs performed during significant market downturns, highlighting key lessons learned and strategies for managing ETFs in turbulent times.

Case Study 1: The 2008 Financial Crisis

Background: The 2008 financial crisis, triggered by the collapse of the housing market and subsequent failures of financial institutions, led to a severe global economic downturn. The stock market experienced significant declines, and many investors sought refuge in less risky assets.

Performance:

- **SPDR S&P 500 ETF (SPY):** As a broad-market ETF tracking the S&P 500, SPY saw substantial declines, mirroring the overall market's drop. From October 2007 to March 2009, the S&P 500 lost about 57% of its value (Investopedia).
- **iShares U.S. Treasury Bond ETF (GOVT):** In contrast, bond ETFs like GOVT, which focus on U.S. Treasury securities, provided stability and even appreciated in value as investors flocked to safer assets.

Lessons Learned:

- **Diversification:** The crisis underscored the importance of diversification, not just within equities but across different asset classes. Bond ETFs played a crucial role in mitigating losses.
- **Risk Management:** Investors learned the value of incorporating less volatile assets, such as bonds, into their portfolios to cushion against severe market downturns.

Case Study 2: The COVID-19 Pandemic

Background: The onset of the COVID-19 pandemic in early 2020 led to unprecedented economic shutdowns and a rapid market sell-off. The stock market experienced extreme volatility, with rapid declines followed by swift recoveries.

Performance:

- **Invesco QQQ ETF (QQQ):** This ETF, which tracks the Nasdaq-100, initially saw sharp declines but quickly rebounded due to the strong performance of technology stocks, which benefitted from the shift to remote work and digital services (Yahoo Finance).
- **iShares iBoxx $ High Yield Corporate Bond ETF (HYG):** High-yield bond ETFs like HYG faced significant stress as the economic impact of the pandemic increased default risks among lower-rated corporate bonds. However, interventions by the Federal Reserve, including the purchase of corporate bonds, helped stabilize this ETF (Bloomberg).

Lessons Learned:

- **Sector Selection:** The pandemic highlighted the importance of sector selection, with technology and healthcare sectors outperforming others.
- **Policy Impact:** The role of government and central bank interventions in stabilizing markets was crucial, particularly for high-yield bonds.

Case Study 3: The 2015-2016 Oil Price Crash

Background: In 2015-2016, global oil prices plummeted due to oversupply and weakening demand, leading to significant losses in the energy sector. This period was marked by high volatility in energy-related assets.

Performance:

- **Energy Select Sector SPDR Fund (XLE):** XLE, which focuses on energy stocks, saw substantial declines as oil prices fell. The ETF lost about 40% of its value from mid-2014 to early 2016 (Morningstar).
- **SPDR Gold Shares ETF (GLD):** As a safe-haven asset, gold and the corresponding GLD ETF saw increased interest, providing stability and diversification benefits during the energy sector turmoil (SSGA).

Lessons Learned:

- **Sector Risks:** The crash demonstrated the risks associated with sector-specific ETFs, particularly in volatile industries like energy.
- **Safe-Haven Assets:** Gold ETFs provided effective hedging and diversification during the sector-specific downturn, emphasizing the role of non-correlated assets in a portfolio.

Conclusion

These case studies illustrate the varied performance of ETFs during different market crises and highlight important lessons for investors. Diversification across asset classes, careful sector selection, and the inclusion of safe-haven assets like bonds and gold can enhance portfolio resilience. By understanding how ETFs have responded to past crises, investors can better prepare for future market volatility.

22. Global ETFs and International Diversification

In an increasingly interconnected world, the benefits of global investing have become more apparent. Global ETFs (Exchange-Traded Funds) provide investors with the opportunity to diversify their portfolios beyond domestic markets, tapping into growth opportunities around the world. By investing in international markets, investors can reduce risk through geographical diversification and gain exposure to different economic cycles, industries, and currencies. This section explores the advantages of global ETFs and the role they play in a well-rounded investment strategy.

22.1 Benefits of International Exposure

1. Diversification Across Economies

Investing internationally allows investors to diversify their portfolios across different economies. This geographical diversification can reduce the overall risk of a portfolio since economic conditions and market performances often vary from one country to another.

- **Example:** During the early 2000s, while the U.S. market experienced a downturn due to the dot-com bubble burst, emerging markets like China and India saw significant economic growth. By including international ETFs, such as the **iShares MSCI Emerging Markets ETF (EEM)**, investors could mitigate losses in the U.S. market with gains from emerging markets (BlackRock).

2. Access to High-Growth Markets

International markets, particularly in emerging economies, often offer higher growth potential compared to developed markets. These regions can provide robust investment opportunities as they industrialize and develop their economies.

- **Example:** The **Vanguard FTSE Emerging Markets ETF (VWO)** gives investors access to fast-growing economies in Asia, Latin America, and Eastern Europe, which have higher growth rates compared to many developed markets (Vanguard).

3. Currency Diversification

Investing in international ETFs introduces currency diversification to a portfolio. Fluctuations in currency exchange rates can impact the returns of international investments, providing both opportunities and risks.

- **Example:** A U.S. investor holding the **iShares MSCI EAFE ETF (EFA)**, which tracks developed markets outside of North America, benefits from exposure to currencies such as the Euro, Yen, and Pound. This can act as a hedge against the weakening of the U.S. dollar (BlackRock).

4. Sector and Industry Diversification

Different countries often have varying sectoral strengths, allowing investors to gain exposure to industries that might be underrepresented in their domestic markets.

- **Example:** The **Global X MSCI SuperDividend EAFE ETF (EFAS)** focuses on high-dividend-yielding companies in Europe, Australasia, and the Far East, providing exposure to sectors like consumer goods and industrials, which might be more dominant in these regions compared to the U.S. (Global X).

5. Potential for Enhanced Returns

By investing in a mix of developed and emerging markets, investors can potentially enhance their returns. Emerging markets, while riskier, often grow at a faster pace, whereas developed markets provide stability.

- **Example:** Combining the **iShares MSCI ACWI ETF (ACWI)**, which includes both developed and emerging markets, with a domestic ETF like the **SPDR S&P 500 ETF (SPY)** can balance the portfolio, offering both growth potential and stability (BlackRock, SSGA).

Conclusion

International diversification through global ETFs offers numerous benefits, including reduced risk through geographical diversification, access to high-growth markets, currency diversification, sector and industry diversification, and the potential for enhanced returns. By incorporating global ETFs into their investment strategies, investors can build more resilient and growth-oriented portfolios, better positioned to navigate the complexities of global financial markets.

References:

1. "Why International Diversification Still Makes Sense" - Vanguard. Vanguard
2. "The Case for Global Diversification" - BlackRock. BlackRock
3. "Global Investing and International ETFs" - Investopedia. Investopedia
4. "MSCI Emerging Markets Index" - MSCI. MSCI

22.2 Types of Global ETFs

Global ETFs offer investors various ways to gain exposure to international markets, ranging from broad-based global funds to those targeting specific regions, countries, or sectors. Understanding the different types of global ETFs can help investors choose the right mix to achieve their diversification goals and enhance their investment portfolios.

1. Broad-Based Global ETFs

These ETFs provide exposure to a wide range of international markets, including both developed and emerging economies. They are designed to offer comprehensive global diversification.

- **Example:** The **iShares MSCI ACWI ETF (ACWI)** tracks the MSCI All Country World Index, covering large and mid-cap stocks across 23 developed and 27 emerging markets (BlackRock).
- **Example:** The **Vanguard Total World Stock ETF (VT)** provides exposure to the entire global equity market, including U.S. and international stocks across all market capitalizations (Vanguard).

2. Regional ETFs

Regional ETFs focus on specific geographical areas, allowing investors to target broader regions rather than individual countries. This can be useful for gaining exposure to economic trends affecting entire regions.

- **Example:** The **SPDR EURO STOXX 50 ETF (FEZ)** targets the Eurozone by tracking the performance of the 50 largest companies in the euro area (SSGA).
- **Example:** The **iShares MSCI Emerging Markets Asia ETF (EEMA)** focuses on emerging Asian markets, offering exposure to countries like China, India, and South Korea (BlackRock).

3. Country-Specific ETFs

Country-specific ETFs invest in companies within a single country, allowing investors to capitalize on the economic prospects of individual nations. These ETFs can be used to take advantage of country-specific opportunities or hedge against risks.

- **Example:** The **iShares MSCI Japan ETF (EWJ)** offers exposure to Japanese stocks, providing access to one of the largest economies in the world (BlackRock).
- **Example:** The **iShares MSCI Brazil ETF (EWZ)** focuses on Brazilian equities, capturing the performance of the largest and most liquid companies in Brazil (BlackRock).

4. Emerging Market ETFs

Emerging market ETFs focus on developing economies, which often offer higher growth potential but come with increased volatility and risk. These ETFs are a way to gain exposure to fast-growing markets.

- **Example:** The **Vanguard FTSE Emerging Markets ETF (VWO)** tracks the performance of large and mid-cap companies in emerging markets such as China, Brazil, and South Africa (Vanguard).
- **Example:** The **iShares MSCI Emerging Markets ETF (EEM)** provides exposure to a broad range of companies in emerging markets around the world (BlackRock).

5. Developed Market ETFs

These ETFs target developed economies, which are typically more stable and less volatile than emerging markets. They are ideal for investors looking for steady growth and lower risk.

- **Example:** The **iShares MSCI EAFE ETF (EFA)** focuses on developed markets outside of North America, including Europe, Australasia, and the Far East (BlackRock).
- **Example:** The **SPDR MSCI World Quality Mix ETF (QWLD)** combines exposure to developed markets with a focus on quality, value, and low volatility factors (SSGA).

6. Sector and Industry-Specific Global ETFs

Sector and industry-specific global ETFs invest in particular sectors or industries across various countries, allowing investors to target global trends in specific areas such as technology, healthcare, or energy.

- **Example:** The **Global X MSCI SuperDividend EAFE ETF (EFAS)** targets high-dividend-yielding companies in developed markets outside of the U.S. and Canada, focusing on sectors like utilities and consumer goods (Global X).
- **Example:** The **iShares Global Tech ETF (IXN)** provides exposure to the global technology sector, including companies like Apple, Samsung, and Microsoft (BlackRock).

Conclusion

Global ETFs come in various forms, each offering unique opportunities for international diversification. From broad-based global funds to specific regional, country, sector, and emerging market ETFs, these investment vehicles allow investors to tailor their portfolios to their risk tolerance and investment objectives. By understanding the different types of global ETFs, investors can strategically diversify their holdings and enhance their potential for long-term growth.

References:

1. "iShares MSCI ACWI ETF (ACWI)" - BlackRock. BlackRock
2. "Vanguard Total World Stock ETF (VT)" - Vanguard. Vanguard
3. "SPDR EURO STOXX 50 ETF (FEZ)" - State Street Global Advisors. SSGA
4. "iShares MSCI Emerging Markets Asia ETF (EEMA)" - BlackRock. BlackRock
5. "iShares MSCI Japan ETF (EWJ)" - BlackRock. BlackRock
6. "iShares MSCI Brazil ETF (EWZ)" - BlackRock. BlackRock
7. "Vanguard FTSE Emerging Markets ETF (VWO)" - Vanguard. Vanguard
8. "iShares MSCI Emerging Markets ETF (EEM)" - BlackRock. BlackRock
9. "iShares MSCI EAFE ETF (EFA)" - BlackRock. BlackRock
10. "Global X MSCI SuperDividend EAFE ETF (EFAS)" - Global X. Global X
11. "iShares Global Tech ETF (IXN)" - BlackRock. BlackRock

22.3 Risks and Considerations

While global ETFs offer significant benefits for diversification and potential growth, they also come with unique risks and considerations that investors need to be aware of. Understanding these risks is crucial for making informed investment decisions and managing a well-balanced portfolio.

1. Currency Risk

Investing in global ETFs exposes investors to currency risk, as the value of foreign investments can be affected by fluctuations in exchange rates. A strengthening domestic currency can erode returns on international investments, while a weakening domestic currency can enhance them.

- **Example:** An investor in the U.S. holding the **iShares MSCI EAFE ETF (EFA)** may see their returns impacted by fluctuations in the Euro, Yen, and other currencies included in the ETF (BlackRock).

Considerations:

- Use currency-hedged ETFs to mitigate currency risk. For example, the **iShares Currency Hedged MSCI EAFE ETF (HEFA)** aims to reduce the impact of currency fluctuations (BlackRock).

2. Political and Economic Risk

Investments in international markets are subject to political and economic risks that can affect market stability and performance. These risks include changes in government, political instability, economic policy shifts, and regulatory changes.

- **Example:** The **iShares MSCI Emerging Markets ETF (EEM)** may be affected by political instability or economic crises in emerging markets like Brazil, India, or China (BlackRock).

Considerations:

- Diversify across multiple regions and countries to spread risk and avoid overconcentration in any single political or economic environment.
- Stay informed about geopolitical developments and economic conditions in the countries where you invest.

3. Market Risk and Volatility

International markets can be more volatile than domestic markets, especially in emerging economies. Market risk includes the potential for significant fluctuations in asset prices due to various factors, including investor sentiment, market liquidity, and economic indicators.

- **Example:** The **Vanguard FTSE Emerging Markets ETF (VWO)** may experience higher volatility due to its exposure to emerging markets, which can be more susceptible to market swings (Vanguard).

Considerations:

- Assess your risk tolerance and adjust your portfolio allocation to international ETFs accordingly.
- Consider incorporating defensive assets, such as bonds or gold ETFs, to balance portfolio volatility.

4. Liquidity Risk

Liquidity risk refers to the difficulty of buying or selling an ETF without significantly impacting its price. Some international markets, particularly those in emerging economies, may have lower liquidity, making it harder to trade large volumes of shares.

- **Example:** The **Global X MSCI SuperDividend EAFE ETF (EFAS)**, which focuses on high-dividend-yielding companies in developed markets, may face liquidity challenges during periods of market stress (Global X).

Considerations:

- Choose ETFs with high average daily trading volumes and robust underlying asset liquidity.
- Monitor the bid-ask spreads of ETFs to gauge liquidity conditions and avoid significant transaction costs.

5. Regulatory and Legal Risk

Different countries have varying regulatory and legal frameworks that can impact investments. Changes in regulations, taxation policies, and legal structures can affect the performance and viability of international ETFs.

- **Example:** The **iShares MSCI Japan ETF (EWJ)** is subject to Japanese regulatory and legal changes that could impact the underlying investments and overall ETF performance (BlackRock).

Considerations:

- Stay updated on international regulatory and legal developments that could affect your investments.
- Consider ETFs that comply with global standards and have transparent governance structures.

6. Information and Transparency Risk

Access to accurate and timely information can be more challenging in international markets, especially in emerging economies. This lack of transparency can lead to increased risk and uncertainty.

- **Example:** The **iShares MSCI Brazil ETF (EWZ)**, which focuses on Brazilian equities, may be affected by information asymmetry and transparency issues within the Brazilian market (BlackRock).

Considerations:

- Invest in ETFs managed by reputable firms with strong track records of providing clear and comprehensive information.
- Utilize financial research tools and resources to stay informed about international markets and investments.

Conclusion

Investing in global ETFs offers substantial opportunities for diversification and growth, but it also involves navigating several risks and considerations. Currency fluctuations, political and economic instability, market volatility, liquidity challenges, regulatory changes, and information asymmetry are critical factors to manage. By understanding these risks and employing strategies such as diversification, currency hedging, and thorough research, investors can effectively incorporate global ETFs into their portfolios to enhance long-term returns.

23. Tax-Loss Harvesting with ETFs

Tax-loss harvesting is a strategic technique that can help investors optimize their tax situations and improve after-tax returns. By selling securities at a loss to offset gains elsewhere in the portfolio, investors can reduce their taxable income. ETFs (Exchange-Traded Funds) are particularly well-suited for this strategy due to their flexibility, diversity, and ease of trading. This section explores the concept of tax-loss harvesting, its benefits, and how to effectively implement it using ETFs.

23.1 What is Tax-Loss Harvesting?

Definition: Tax-loss harvesting is an investment strategy where investors sell securities at a loss to offset capital gains from other investments. This process reduces the overall tax liability for the investor. The harvested losses can be used to offset gains and, in some cases, up to $3,000 of ordinary income per year for individual filers or $1,500 for married couples filing separately.

How It Works:

- **Sell Losing Investments:** Identify investments that have declined in value and sell them to realize the losses.
- **Offset Gains:** Use the realized losses to offset any capital gains from other investments within the same tax year.
- **Repurchase Similar Investments:** Reinvest the proceeds in similar but not identical securities to maintain the desired asset allocation and market exposure while avoiding the IRS wash-sale rule, which disallows the deduction if the same or substantially identical security is purchased within 30 days before or after the sale.

Example:

- Suppose an investor holds shares in the **Vanguard Total Stock Market ETF (VTI)** and it has declined in value. The investor can sell VTI to realize a loss and then purchase a similar but not identical

ETF, such as the **iShares Core S&P Total U.S. Stock Market ETF (ITOT)**, to maintain exposure to the U.S. stock market while capturing the tax benefit (Vanguard, BlackRock).

Benefits:

- **Tax Efficiency:** By offsetting gains with losses, investors can lower their taxable income, potentially resulting in significant tax savings.
- **Portfolio Rebalancing:** Tax-loss harvesting provides an opportunity to review and rebalance the portfolio, ensuring it aligns with long-term investment goals.
- **Enhanced Returns:** The tax savings achieved through tax-loss harvesting can enhance after-tax returns, improving overall portfolio performance.

Considerations:

- **Wash-Sale Rule:** Investors must be aware of the wash-sale rule, which disallows the tax deduction if the same or substantially identical security is repurchased within 30 days. To comply, investors should select alternative investments that provide similar market exposure without violating this rule.
- **Market Timing:** The strategy involves selling securities at a loss, which requires careful consideration of market conditions and timing to avoid locking in losses that could recover in the short term.

23.2 How to Implement It with ETFs

Implementing tax-loss harvesting with ETFs involves several strategic steps that help investors minimize their tax liabilities while maintaining their investment goals. Here's a detailed guide on how to effectively implement tax-loss harvesting using ETFs.

Step 1: Identify Eligible ETFs for Tax-Loss Harvesting

- **Review Your Portfolio:** Regularly review your portfolio to identify ETFs that have declined in value. Focus on those that have significant unrealized losses.
- **Example:** Suppose you hold the **SPDR S&P 500 ETF (SPY)**, and it has declined significantly over the year. This ETF could be a candidate for tax-loss harvesting (SSGA).

Step 2: Calculate Potential Losses

- **Determine Loss Amount:** Calculate the difference between the purchase price and the current market value of the ETFs to determine the potential loss.
- **Example:** If you purchased **SPY** at $350 per share and it is now trading at $300 per share, the loss per share would be $50.

Step 3: Sell the Losing ETFs

- **Execute the Sale:** Sell the identified ETFs to realize the losses. Ensure that the sale is executed in a taxable account, as tax-loss harvesting does not apply to tax-advantaged accounts like IRAs or 401(k)s.
- **Example:** Sell your shares of **SPY** to lock in the $50 per share loss.

Step 4: Offset Gains

- **Offset Capital Gains:** Use the realized losses to offset any capital gains within the same tax year. If your losses exceed your gains, you can use up to $3,000 of the excess loss to offset ordinary income ($1,500 if married filing separately).
- **Example:** If you have $10,000 in capital gains from other investments, and you realize $5,000 in losses from selling **SPY**, you can offset those gains, reducing your taxable income by $5,000.

Step 5: Reinvest in Similar, Not Identical ETFs

- **Avoid the Wash-Sale Rule:** To maintain market exposure and comply with the wash-sale rule, reinvest the proceeds in a similar but not identical ETF. The wash-sale rule disallows the deduction if

you buy the same or substantially identical security within 30 days before or after the sale.
- **Example:** After selling **SPY**, you could purchase the **iShares Core S&P 500 ETF (IVV)**, which tracks the same index but is not considered identical (BlackRock).

Step 6: Maintain Portfolio Balance

- **Review Asset Allocation:** Ensure that the new investments maintain the overall asset allocation and investment strategy of your portfolio.
- **Example:** If your portfolio strategy is to have 60% in U.S. equities, ensure that the new ETF, like **IVV**, keeps you aligned with this strategy.

Step 7: Document Transactions

- **Keep Detailed Records:** Document all transactions, including the purchase dates, sale dates, amounts, and prices. This documentation is essential for tax reporting and compliance.
- **Example:** Maintain a spreadsheet or use portfolio management software to track your tax-loss harvesting activities.

Considerations and Best Practices:

- **Regular Reviews:** Conduct regular portfolio reviews, especially towards the end of the tax year, to identify potential tax-loss harvesting opportunities.
- **Professional Advice:** Consider consulting with a tax professional or financial advisor to optimize your tax-loss harvesting strategy and ensure compliance with tax laws.
- **Long-Term Focus:** While tax-loss harvesting provides short-term tax benefits, ensure that your investment decisions align with your long-term financial goals and risk tolerance.

Conclusion

Tax-loss harvesting with ETFs is an effective strategy to reduce tax liabilities and improve after-tax returns. By identifying eligible ETFs, calculating potential losses, executing sales, reinvesting in similar but not identical ETFs, and maintaining portfolio balance, investors can optimize their tax situations while adhering to their overall investment strategy. Regular reviews and professional advice can further enhance the effectiveness of this approach.

23.3 Benefits and Pitfalls

Tax-loss harvesting with ETFs can be a highly effective strategy for reducing tax liabilities and enhancing after-tax returns. However, like any investment strategy, it comes with its own set of benefits and pitfalls. Understanding these can help investors make informed decisions and maximize the effectiveness of their tax-loss harvesting efforts.

Benefits

1. **Reduction of Tax Liability**
- **Offsetting Gains:** One of the primary benefits of tax-loss harvesting is the ability to offset capital gains with realized losses. This can significantly reduce an investor's taxable income for the year.
    - **Example:** If an investor realizes $10,000 in capital gains but also realizes $10,000 in losses through tax-loss harvesting, their net capital gain is zero, thus eliminating their capital gains tax for that year (Vanguard).
- **Ordinary Income Offset:** Up to $3,000 of net capital losses can be used to offset ordinary income each year ($1,500 if married filing separately), which can result in substantial tax savings.
    - **Example:** An investor with $3,000 in net capital losses can reduce their taxable ordinary income by $3,000, potentially lowering their overall tax bracket (Investopedia).
2. **Improved After-Tax Returns**

- **Reinvestment:** By reinvesting the proceeds from sold ETFs into similar but not identical investments, investors can maintain their market exposure and investment strategy while capturing the tax benefits.
    - **Example:** After selling the **SPDR S&P 500 ETF (SPY)** at a loss, an investor can buy the **iShares Core S&P 500 ETF (IVV)** to stay invested in the U.S. stock market (BlackRock).

3. **Portfolio Rebalancing**
- **Regular Review:** Tax-loss harvesting encourages regular portfolio review, which can lead to better asset allocation and alignment with long-term investment goals.
    - **Example:** Regularly assessing ETFs for potential losses and gains helps investors maintain a balanced and well-diversified portfolio (Charles Schwab).

4. **Compounding Tax Savings**
- **Long-Term Benefits:** The tax savings realized through tax-loss harvesting can be reinvested, leading to compounded growth over time.
    - **Example:** Using tax savings to purchase additional investments can enhance the portfolio's growth potential, leading to higher overall returns (Morningstar).

Pitfalls

1. **Wash-Sale Rule**
- **IRS Regulations:** The wash-sale rule disallows the deduction of a loss if a substantially identical security is purchased within 30 days before or after the sale. This can complicate the tax-loss harvesting strategy and requires careful planning.
    - **Example:** If an investor sells **SPY** and repurchases it within 30 days, the loss cannot be claimed for tax purposes (Investopedia).

2. **Market Timing Risks**
- **Short-Term Market Movements:** Selling investments at a loss to capture tax benefits can lead to locking in losses that might have otherwise recovered if held longer.

- **Example:** An investor might sell an ETF at a low point only to see it rebound shortly after, resulting in missed recovery gains (Vanguard).
3. **Increased Trading Costs**
- **Transaction Fees:** Frequent buying and selling of ETFs can result in higher transaction costs, which can eat into the tax savings achieved through tax-loss harvesting.
    - **Example:** Commission fees, bid-ask spreads, and other trading costs can add up, reducing the net benefit of the strategy (Charles Schwab).
4. **Complexity in Record-Keeping**
- **Detailed Documentation:** Tax-loss harvesting requires meticulous record-keeping to track purchase dates, sale dates, amounts, and prices to comply with tax regulations.
    - **Example:** Maintaining accurate records of all transactions and wash-sale implications can be time-consuming and complex (Morningstar).
5. **Short-Term vs. Long-Term Goals**
- **Potential Distraction:** Focusing too much on short-term tax benefits can distract from long-term investment goals, leading to suboptimal portfolio management.
    - **Example:** Investors might prioritize tax savings over sound investment principles, potentially undermining their long-term financial strategy (Investopedia).

Conclusion

Tax-loss harvesting with ETFs offers significant benefits, including reduced tax liabilities, improved after-tax returns, and enhanced portfolio management. However, it also presents challenges such as adherence to the wash-sale rule, market timing risks, increased trading costs, and the need for detailed record-keeping. By carefully weighing these benefits and pitfalls, investors can effectively implement tax-loss harvesting to optimize their tax situations while staying aligned with their long-term investment goals.

24. Understanding ETF Fees and Expenses

Exchange-Traded Funds (ETFs) are often praised for their cost-efficiency compared to mutual funds, making them an attractive option for many investors. However, like any investment vehicle, ETFs come with their own set of fees and expenses that can impact overall returns. Understanding these costs is crucial for making informed investment decisions and maximizing the benefits of investing in ETFs. This section will explore the different types of fees associated with ETFs and how they affect investment performance.

24.1 Different Types of Fees

Investors should be aware of several types of fees when investing in ETFs, each affecting the net returns in different ways. These fees can be broadly categorized into management fees, trading costs, and other expenses.

1. Management Fees

Management fees, often represented by the expense ratio, are the most visible and commonly discussed costs associated with ETFs. This fee compensates the fund manager for managing the fund's portfolio and is expressed as an annual percentage of the fund's average assets under management (AUM).

- **Expense Ratio:** This is the annual fee that all ETF investors must pay. It covers the fund's operating expenses, including management fees, administrative fees, and other operational costs. The expense ratio is deducted from the fund's assets, reducing the returns to investors.
    - **Example:** If an ETF has an expense ratio of 0.10%, this means that for every $1,000 invested, $1 will be deducted annually to cover management and operational costs (Investopedia, Morningstar).

2. Trading Costs

Trading costs include all the expenses associated with buying and selling ETF shares. These can vary based on the frequency of trades, the brokerage platform used, and the bid-ask spread.

- **Commissions:** Some brokerages charge a commission every time you buy or sell ETF shares. While many brokerages have moved to commission-free trading, it's important to confirm the fee structure of your specific brokerage.
    - **Example:** If a brokerage charges $5 per trade, buying and then selling an ETF would incur a total of $10 in commissions (Charles Schwab, Fidelity).
- **Bid-Ask Spread:** The bid-ask spread is the difference between the highest price a buyer is willing to pay for an ETF (bid) and the lowest price a seller is willing to accept (ask). This spread can be a hidden cost of trading, especially for ETFs with lower liquidity.
    - **Example:** An ETF with a bid price of $50.00 and an ask price of $50.05 has a bid-ask spread of $0.05. Frequent trading in ETFs with wide spreads can add up to significant costs over time (Investopedia).

3. Additional Expenses

Other less obvious fees can also impact the total cost of owning an ETF.

- **Securities Lending Revenue:** Some ETFs lend out securities to other institutions for a fee. While this can generate additional revenue for the fund, there is also a risk involved. The revenue from securities lending can help offset some of the fund's expenses, but it is not guaranteed.
    - **Example:** An ETF that engages in securities lending might generate extra income, which can help reduce the effective expense ratio for investors (Morningstar).
- **Tracking Error:** This is the difference between the ETF's performance and the performance of its benchmark index. A significant tracking error can indicate higher indirect costs and inefficiencies within the fund.

ETFs, dangerous financial instruments?

- **Example:** If an ETF tracking the S&P 500 has a tracking error of 0.5%, it means the ETF underperformed or outperformed the index by 0.5%, which can be seen as an indirect cost to investors (ETF.com).

Conclusion

Understanding the different types of fees associated with ETFs is essential for investors looking to maximize their returns. Management fees, trading costs, and other expenses can all impact the overall cost of owning ETFs. By being aware of these fees and factoring them into investment decisions, investors can make more informed choices and better achieve their financial goals.

References:

1. "Understanding ETF Fees and Expenses" - Investopedia. Investopedia
2. "ETF Expense Ratio: What It Is and Why It Matters" - Morningstar. Morningstar
3. "The True Cost of ETF Investing" - Charles Schwab. Charles Schwab
4. "Understanding the Bid-Ask Spread" - Fidelity. Fidelity

24.2 Impact on Long-Term Returns

The impact of fees and expenses on long-term returns is a critical consideration for ETF investors. Even seemingly small fees can compound over time, significantly reducing the overall performance of an investment. Understanding this impact helps investors make informed decisions that align with their financial goals.

1. The Compounding Effect of Fees

Management fees and other expenses, represented by the ETF's expense ratio, are deducted from the fund's assets. This deduction reduces the amount of money that can be reinvested, leading to lower compounding growth over time.

- **Example:** Suppose an investor places $10,000 in an ETF with an annual return of 7% and an expense ratio of 0.1%. Over 20 years, the investment grows to $36,719. With an expense ratio of 1%, the same investment grows to only $32,071. The higher expense ratio reduces the final amount by $4,648 due to the compounding effect of the fees (Investopedia).

2. Impact on Different Types of Investors

- **Long-Term Investors:** Investors with a long investment horizon, such as those saving for retirement, are more affected by high expense ratios. The longer the investment period, the greater the impact of fees on overall returns.
    - **Example:** Over 30 years, an ETF with a 0.1% expense ratio versus one with a 1% expense ratio can result in a significant difference in returns. The lower-cost ETF will preserve more capital, leading to higher compounding growth (Morningstar).
- **Short-Term Investors:** While short-term investors are less impacted by fees due to the shorter compounding period, trading costs like commissions and bid-ask spreads can still affect their returns, especially if they trade frequently.
    - **Example:** Frequent trading in ETFs with wide bid-ask spreads or high commissions can erode short-term gains, making cost efficiency crucial even for short-term strategies (Charles Schwab).

3. Case Study: Comparing Low-Cost and High-Cost ETFs

- **Low-Cost ETF:** The **Vanguard Total Stock Market ETF (VTI)** has a low expense ratio of 0.03%. Over 20 years, assuming an average annual return of 7%, a $10,000 investment grows to approximately $38,696.
- **High-Cost ETF:** A comparable high-cost ETF with a 1% expense ratio would see the same $10,000 investment grow to only $30,182

over the same period, assuming the same 7% return before fees. The high-cost ETF underperforms by $8,514 due to higher fees (Vanguard, Morningstar).

4. Total Cost Consideration

When evaluating the impact of fees on long-term returns, it's essential to consider all associated costs, including:

- **Expense Ratio:** The ongoing annual fee deducted from the fund's assets.
- **Trading Costs:** Commissions and bid-ask spreads incurred during buying and selling.
- **Tracking Error:** The discrepancy between the ETF's performance and its benchmark, which can indicate additional indirect costs.

5. Strategies to Minimize Fee Impact

- **Choose Low-Cost ETFs:** Opt for ETFs with low expense ratios to maximize compounding returns.
- **Limit Trading:** Reduce the frequency of trades to minimize commissions and bid-ask spread costs.
- **Monitor Tracking Error:** Select ETFs with minimal tracking error to ensure they closely follow their benchmarks, avoiding additional hidden costs.

Conclusion

Fees and expenses have a profound impact on long-term ETF returns due to their compounding effect. By understanding and minimizing these costs, investors can significantly enhance their portfolio's performance over time. Choosing low-cost ETFs, limiting trading, and monitoring tracking errors are effective strategies to mitigate the negative impact of fees, ensuring that more of the investment's growth is retained.

24.3 Comparing ETF Costs

When selecting ETFs for your investment portfolio, comparing costs is crucial to maximizing your long-term returns. Various cost components can significantly impact the overall performance of your investment. Here's how to effectively compare ETF costs:

1. Expense Ratios

The expense ratio is the primary cost associated with ETFs, representing the annual fee as a percentage of assets under management.

- **Low-Cost Leaders:** Some ETFs are known for their exceptionally low expense ratios. For example, the **Vanguard Total Stock Market ETF (VTI)** has an expense ratio of 0.03%, making it one of the most cost-effective options in the market (Vanguard).
- **Industry Averages:** According to Morningstar, the average expense ratio for ETFs is around 0.44%. Comparatively, mutual funds have higher average expense ratios, often around 1% or more (Morningstar).

2. Trading Costs

Trading costs include commissions and bid-ask spreads incurred when buying and selling ETF shares.

- **Commission-Free Trading:** Many brokerages now offer commission-free trading for ETFs, including firms like Charles Schwab, Fidelity, and Vanguard. This significantly reduces the cost of frequent trading (Charles Schwab, Fidelity).
- **Bid-Ask Spreads:** The bid-ask spread can be a hidden cost. For example, highly liquid ETFs like the **SPDR S&P 500 ETF (SPY)** typically have narrow spreads, while less liquid ETFs may have wider spreads, increasing the trading cost (SSGA).

3. Tracking Error

Tracking error measures how closely an ETF follows its benchmark index. A higher tracking error indicates less efficient tracking, potentially leading to lower returns.

- **Low Tracking Error Examples:** ETFs like the **iShares Core S&P 500 ETF (IVV)** often have low tracking errors due to their efficient management and high liquidity, closely following the S&P 500 Index (BlackRock).

4. Securities Lending Revenue

Some ETFs engage in securities lending to generate additional revenue, which can offset some of the fund's expenses.

- **Revenue Sharing:** Funds that lend out securities and share the revenue with investors can effectively reduce the net expense ratio. It's essential to check if an ETF engages in this practice and how the revenue is shared.

5. Total Cost Consideration

When comparing ETF costs, it's important to consider the total cost of ownership, including both direct and indirect costs.

- **Example Comparison:**
    - **Vanguard Total Stock Market ETF (VTI):** Expense ratio of 0.03%, low bid-ask spread, and no commission at major brokerages.
    - **iShares Russell 2000 ETF (IWM):** Expense ratio of 0.19%, generally higher bid-ask spread due to less liquidity compared to large-cap ETFs, and potential trading costs if not using a commission-free brokerage (BlackRock).

Comparing ETF costs involves evaluating expense ratios, trading costs, tracking errors, and any additional revenue offsets such as securities lending. By focusing on these key factors, investors can choose cost-effective ETFs that align with their investment strategy and financial goals. Minimizing these costs is crucial to enhancing long-term returns and achieving financial success.

***

Conclusion : Practical Applications

In this part, we have delved into practical strategies and considerations for effective ETF investing. From building a diversified portfolio and adapting to different market conditions to understanding the nuances of ETF fees and implementing tax-loss harvesting, we've covered essential aspects to enhance your investment journey. By applying these strategies, you can optimize your portfolio, manage risks more effectively, and ultimately work towards achieving your long-term financial objectives. Remember, informed decision-making and regular portfolio reviews are key to navigating the dynamic world of ETFs successfully.

Conclusion

25. ETFs: Final Thoughts

25.1 Summary of benefits and risks

Exchange-Traded Funds (ETFs) have established themselves as popular and versatile financial instruments, appealing to both novice investors and seasoned professionals. However, like any investment tool, they have both benefits and risks that should be weighed carefully.

Advantages of ETFs

The advantages of ETFs are multiple and well documented. They offer a **instant diversification** by allowing investors to purchase a basket of assets in a single transaction. For example, an ETF tracking the S&P 500 provides access to the 500 largest US companies, thereby spreading risk across a broad base (Investopedia).

THE **reduced management fees** are another major asset. Unlike mutual funds, ETFs generally have lower annual fees, often below 0.20%, as is the case with the Schwab U.S. Broad Market ETF (SCHB) (NerdWallet). This means more of your winnings stay in your pocket.

ETFs also offer **great trading flexibility**, trading like stocks throughout the day at prices that fluctuate in real time. This feature allows investors to react quickly to market movements, adding a layer of dynamism to their investment strategy (Investopedia).

Finally, ETFs benefit from a **tax efficiency** superior thanks to their unique creation and redemption structure, thereby minimizing distributions of taxable capital gains (Wall Street Survivor).

Risks of ETFs

Despite their many advantages, ETFs also carry risks that should not be overlooked. There **market volatility** may affect the performance of ETFs, particularly those that track sector or emerging market indices. For example, ETFs based on commodities or technologies can experience significant fluctuations depending on economic conditions and sector regulations (Business Insider).

THE **liquidity risks** are another concern, especially for less popular ETFs or those investing in less liquid assets. Low liquidity can result in wider price spreads and higher transaction costs, making it difficult to buy or sell shares at a reasonable price (Morningstar).

THE **tracking errors** (tracking errors) also represent a challenge. These errors arise when the ETF fails to accurately replicate the performance of its benchmark, often due to management costs and transaction fees. A good example is the SPDR Gold Shares (GLD), which can sometimes deviate from the actual gold price performance (Investopedia).

**

ETFs offer an attractive blend of diversification, low fees, flexibility and tax efficiency, making them a smart choice for many investors. However, it is crucial to understand the associated risks, such as market volatility, liquidity issues and tracking errors, in order to carefully navigate this financial world. As with any investment, the key lies in careful assessment and proactive risk management. Ultimately, ETFs can be powerful allies in the quest for financial returns, provided they are used wisely and strategically.

25.2 Future Outlook of ETFs

ETFs have revolutionized the world of investing since their introduction in the 1990s, and they continue to grow and evolve at an impressive pace.

ETFs, dangerous financial instruments?

Let's explore the emerging trends and future prospects of these financial instruments with hard facts to inform our thinking.

1. The rise of active ETFs

Historically, ETFs were primarily associated with passive management strategies, but active ETFs are taking an increasing share of the market. In 2023, active ETFs represented about 6% of total ETF assets in the United States, but they have attracted almost 24% of inflows year-to-date. This trend is fueled by growing demand for differentiated investment strategies and products that meet environmental, social and governance (ESG) criteria (Capital Group).

2. Product innovation and diversity

ETFs continue to diversify with the introduction of innovative products such as thematic ETFs, which focus on specific sectors such as artificial intelligence, cybersecurity and renewable energy. These ETFs allow investors to capture long-term growth trends and gain exposure to promising sectors. For example, ETFs such as the Global

3. Global Expansion and Increased Adoption

The ETF market continues to grow globally. In the United States, ETF assets under management reached $7.3 trillion in September 2023, compared to $4.3 trillion before the pandemic. In Europe, the adoption of ETFs follows the American trend, with a significant increase in new fund launches. In 2022, around 70% of new funds launched in the United States were ETFs, a figure that illustrates their growing popularity (Oliver Wyman).

4. Tax benefits and efficiency

The tax advantages of ETFs, including their efficient structure that minimizes capital gains distributions, continue to attract investors. In the United States, favorable regulations, such as the SEC's 2019 ETF rule, have enabled increased competition and rapid expansion of the ETF market (Investopedia).

5. Expected growth in assets under management

Forecasts for the next few years are optimistic. Global ETF assets under management are expected to reach at least $18 trillion by 2026, with annual growth forecast between 13% and 18%, according to a PwC survey. This growth is driven by the continued influx of capital, the arrival of new players on the market and the development of innovative products (PwC).

***

The future outlook for ETFs is bright, with continued innovation and growing adoption across the globe. The rise of active ETFs, product diversification, tax benefits and global expansion are all factors supporting this growth. Investors must stay informed of emerging trends and new opportunities to make the most of these dynamic financial instruments. Like any good TV series, the best is yet to come for ETFs, and it's worth staying tuned to see how this story unfolds.

Annexes

26. Glossary of Key Terms

Navigating the world of ETFs can sometimes be like deciphering a secret language. Here is a glossary of key terms to help you become a true financial polyglot.

Assets Under Management (AUM)

It is the total value of assets that an ETF manages on behalf of its investors. Think of this as the total amount of money in a financial superhero's wallet. The higher the AUM, the more stable and liquid the ETF generally is.

Management Fees (TER - Total Expense Ratio)

This annual fee covers the costs of managing the ETF. Think of it like subscription fees for Netflix, except you're hoping your ETF earns you more than a new season of "Stranger Things."

Liquidity

The ease with which an ETF can be bought or sold without affecting its price. Good liquidity means you can exit your investment as quickly as a teenager exits TikTok at dinner time.

Physical Replica vs. Synthetic Replica

Physical replication means that the ETF directly owns the underlying assets of the index it tracks. It's like buying a vinyl album from your favorite band – you have the record in your hand. Synthetic cueing, on the other hand, uses swaps to mimic the index's performance, much like listening to a streaming playlist: you have the music, but not the record.

Tracking Error

ETFs, dangerous financial instruments?

The difference between the performance of the ETF and that of its benchmark index. Low tracking error is like a song perfectly synchronized with the choreography of a music video – everything lines up perfectly.

Dividend

A distribution of profits by a corporation to shareholders. For ETFs, this means receiving a share of the profits of the companies in which the ETF invests. It's like getting a piece of the birthday cake even if you didn't help make it.

Exposition

The percentage of an ETF's assets invested in a specific market or sector. Large exposure to technology, for example, means the ETF is heavily invested in technology companies. That's like saying your Spotify playlist is dominated by Korean pop.

Ratio de Rotation (Turnover Ratio)

The percentage of a portfolio that is replaced during a given period. A high turnover ratio indicates a lot of trading activity, much like changing your clothing look every week.

NAV (Net Asset Value)

The value per share of the ETF, calculated by dividing the total value of assets by the number of shares outstanding. It's the financial equivalent of knowing the average price per slice of a cake you've baked.

Spread

The difference between the buy price (ask) and the sell price (bid) of an ETF. A tight spread is ideal and means you don't lose too much money buying or selling. It's like finding the same item at the same price in two different stores – no need to run around for the best deal.

ETF Inverse

An ETF designed to gain value when the index it tracks loses value. He's the superhero who thrives in tough times, much like Batman who thrives in darkness.

Leveraged ETF

These ETFs use derivatives to amplify the returns of the index being tracked, often by a factor of two or three. They're powerful but risky, a bit like a Lamborghini – exciting to drive, but only for those who know what they're doing.

This glossary should make your exploration of ETFs as seamless as navigating your favorite streaming app. For more information, resources like Investopedia and ETF.com offer detailed definitions and educational articles.

27. Additional Resources

For those who wish to deepen their understanding of ETFs and investing in general, here is a list of recommended books, articles and websites, be careful one or two intruders have integrated themselves into this list to make the journey more pleasant for you.

Books

1. "The Bogleheads' Guide to Investing" de Taylor Larimore, Mel Lindauer et Michael LeBoeuf
    - This book is a must-read introduction to common-sense investing principles, inspired by the teachings of John C. Bogle, the founder of Vanguard.
2. "A Random Walk Down Wall Street" de Burton G. Malkiel
    - A classic that explains the concepts of passive investing and why it is often preferable to active management.
3. "ETF Trading and Investing Strategies" de David Vomund

ETFs, dangerous financial instruments?

- This book provides practical strategies for getting the most out of ETFs in various market contexts.
4. **"Investing in Unicorns and Other Mythological Creatures" by Dr. U. R. Kidding**
    - A humorous, fictional exploration of investing in imaginary businesses, a reminder that not all opportunities are what they seem.

Articles

1. **"The Rise of ETFs: Benefits and Risks" - Investopedia**
    - A comprehensive article covering the rise of ETFs, their benefits and associated risks. Link to article[42]
2. **"How to Choose the Right ETF for Your Portfolio" - NerdWallet**
    - A practical guide to selecting the ETFs that best match your investment objectives. Link to article[43]
3. **"ETFs in Wonderland: Investing Beyond the Looking Glass" - Alice F. Wonderland**
    - A satirical article on the potential pitfalls of investing, especially when blindly following trends. Link to article[44]

Sites Web

1. **ETF.com**
    - A leading resource for ETF reviews and comparisons, offering tools to filter and evaluate funds based on various criteria. Link to site[45]
2. **Morningstar**
    - Provides detailed reviews, star ratings and in-depth analysis of ETFs and mutual funds. Link to site[46]
3. **YCharts**

---

[42] https://www.investopedia.com

[43] https://www.nerdwallet.com

[44] https://www.financialwonderland.com

[45] https://www.etf.com

[46] https://www.morningstar.com

- Offers advanced tools to analyze ETF performance, compare fees and assess risk. Link to site[47]
4. **"The Annual Report on Time-Travel ETFs" - FutureInvest**
   - A fictional and humorous site which offers analyzes on theoretical ETFs allowing you to invest in the past and the future. Perfect for reminding you of the importance of remaining realistic in your investment expectations. Link to site[48]

By combining these resources, you will be well equipped to navigate the complex world of ETFs with confidence and insight.

28. Bibliography

Here is a list of cited sources and recommendations for further reading, which provide valuable insights into ETFs and investment strategies.

Sources Cited

1. **Investopedia**
   - Articles on the benefits and risks of ETFs, as well as portfolio management strategies.
   - Investopedia[49]
2. **Morningstar**
   - Detailed analyzes and star ratings of ETFs and mutual funds.
   - Morningstar[50]
3. **NerdWallet**
   - Practical guides on selecting ETFs and comparing fees.
   - NerdWallet[51]
4. **ETF.com**

---

[47] https://www.ycharts.com
[48] https://www.futureinvestfiction.com
[49] https://www.investopedia.com
[50] https://www.morningstar.com
[51] https://www.nerdwallet.com

- Comprehensive resource for ETF analysis and comparisons.
- ETF[52].with

5. **YCharts**
   - Advanced tools to analyze ETF performance and assess risk.
   - YCharts[53]

6. **Wall Street Survivor**
   - Educational articles on mutual funds and investment strategies.
   - Wall Street Survivor[54]

7. **Finance Strategists**
   - Comparison between ETFs and index funds.
   - Finance Strategists[55]

8. **Business Insider**
   - Market analyzes and case studies on ETFs.
   - Business Insider[56]

9. **PwC**
   - Reports on ETF future prospects and market trends.
   - PwC[57]

10. **BlackRock**
    - Information on ETF products and thematic investment trends.
    - BlackRock[58]

---

[52] https://www.etf.com
[53] https://www.ycharts.com
[54] https://www.wallstreetsurvivor.com
[55] https://www.financestrategists.com
[56] https://www.businessinsider.com
[57] https://www.pwc.com
[58] https://www.blackrock.com

www.ingramcontent.com/pod-product-compliance
Lightning Source LLC
Chambersburg PA
CBHW071830210526
45479CB00001B/72